PLAYS THAT TRIP YOU UP

THE BASEBALL UMPIRES HANDBOOK

BY JEFFREY STERN & MATT MORRE

FROM *REFEREE* MAGAZINE & THE NATIONAL ASSOCIATION OF SPORTS OFFICIALS

Plays That Trip You Up:
The Baseball Umpires Handbook

By Jeffrey Stern, senior editor, *Referee*/NASO;
and Matt Moore, associate editor, *Referee*/NASO

Graphics and layout by Ross Bray, graphic designer, *Referee* magazine

Published by Referee Enterprises, Inc., and the National Association of Sports Officials.

Printed in the United States of America

ISBN-13: 978-1-58208-138-0

CONTENTS

INTRODUCTION

Based on television ratings, merchandise sales and attendance figures, it appears football has replaced baseball as America's Pastime. Well, this is one American who cannot help but recall the statement, "There are liars, damned liars and statistics."

Forget the numbers. Baseball is and always will be part of the fabric of this nation. It has the richest history and has produced some of the most dramatic and memorable moments in the annals of sports. It will always be America's game.

It is also one of the more challenging sports to officiate. The plate umpire in a game may make more than 250 decisions in a two-hour period of time: ball, strike, balk, hit batter, safe, out, fair, foul. And while a base umpire may not be challenged nearly as often, there is always that catch/trap, whacker at first or obstruction/interference call waiting to reach up and bite.

This book is intended to help you with the calls that go beyond balls and strikes, safes and outs, fair balls and foul balls. They are the situations that may happen once a game, once a week or once a season. Get them wrong and you'll find yourself in a jam. Get them right, and you'll enhance your reputation among coaches, players, assigners, supervisors and fellow umpires.

The book includes NFHS and NCAA rules, since those are the ones most umpires of amateur baseball will be following. The caseplays have been previously published or were written by *Referee*.

A great many people contributed their knowledge and talents to this book. Chief among them are *Referee* baseball editor Matt Moore; veteran umpires and longtime *Referee* contributors George Demetriou, Colorado Springs, Colo., and Jay Miner, Albany, N.Y.; and Rick Roder, umpire and author from Remsen, Iowa.

The fact you bought this book is much appreciated. But beyond that, as fellow umpires, we appreciate the fact that you want to become a better umpire. Thanks for helping our great avocation.

Jeffrey Stern
Senior editor
Referee magazine

CHAPTER 1

APPEALS

An appeal is the act of a fielder or coach claiming a violation of the rules by the opposing team. There are three main types of appeals — baserunning infractions (missed base, as seen in PlayPic A, or left too early), batting out of order and checked swings. For now, we'll focus on baserunning appeals.

Appeals for baserunning infractions must be made while the ball is live in NCAA, but may also be made while the ball is dead in NFHS.

Appeal plays on runners may involve missing a base, failing to properly retouch a base (leaving too soon) or failing to touch home immediately after

PlayPic®
A

Be alert for a runner who misses a base.

overrunning/oversliding. In NCAA, a runner who takes a running start on a tag up must also be appealed, but in NFHS such a runner is immediately declared out.

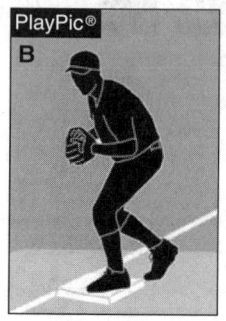

Stepping on a base or tagging a runner are methods of appealing a missed base.

An appeal must be clearly intended as an appeal, either by a verbal request or an act that unmistakably indicates an appeal to the umpire. A player inadvertently stepping on a base with the ball in hand (accidental appeal) does not constitute an appeal. On an appeal play, the fielder may tag the base missed or left too soon (PlayPic B) or the runner (PlayPic C).

If there possibly is more than one runner involved in an appeal at a base, the defensive team must declare on which runner the appeal is being made. If the defensive team fails to identify such runner, the umpire shall give no signal or ask which runner is being appealed.

STATUS OF THE BALL

The NFHS has greatly simplified the appeal process. The traditional live-ball appeal required by NCAA rules need not be used. After a play ends, if the ball is dead, a defensive player, with or without the ball, or a coach may make an appeal by verbally stating the infraction.

In NCAA play, appeals must be made while the ball is live. The same procedure is used in NFHS before the ball is declared dead. If the ball has been declared dead after the infraction, it must first be made live by the umpire. Play is resumed when the pitcher takes his place on the pitcher's plate with a new ball or the same ball in his possession and the runners have reached the bases to which they are entitled or retouched their bases. The plate umpire then points to the pitcher and puts the ball in play. An invalid appeal with a dead ball does not cancel the right to appeal.

STATUTE OF LIMITATIONS

An appeal may be made before the next pitch or any play or attempted play by the defense. So if the defense is ready to appeal but a baserunner attempts to steal before the appeal can be made, the defense does not lose the right to appeal after making a play on the would-be base stealer.

If the infraction occurs during a play that ends a half-inning or the game, the appeal must be made before the defensive team leaves the field. That means before the pitcher and all infielders have crossed the foul lines and before the catcher has left his position on the way to the bench.

APPEAL NEGATED

If the defense initiates a play (such as a pickoff attempt), the opportunity to appeal is lost. If a pitcher balks when making an appeal, it is considered a play and no further appeals are allowed. It is not a balk for a pitcher, while in contact with the rubber (does not step back), to throw to an unoccupied base for the purpose of making an appeal.

If the pitcher or any member of the defensive team throws the ball out of play when making an appeal, it is considered an attempted play and no further appeals are allowed on any runner at any base.

That problem can be avoided in NFHS play, because the rules permit the dead-ball appeal.

If the erroneous throw on an appeal remains in live-ball territory, the appeal is allowed if the ball immediately is returned to the base being appealed and no runners advance on the misplay. However in NCAA, if any runner advances, the appeal is not allowed.

FOURTH OUT APPEAL

An appeal may require a fourth out to be recognized. If the third out is made prior to a valid appeal play, the appeal play decision takes precedence in determining the third out, thus nullifying runs that may have been scored. If there is more than one appeal in such a situation, the defense may choose the most advantageous out.

RETOUCHING A MISSED BASE

Almost any time a runner fails to touch a base, he can return to that base and make his advance around the basepaths legal as long as the ball remains live.

There is, however, one notable exception to that thought — once a following runner has scored, a preceding runner can no longer return to touch any base.

In MechaniGram A, R2 has attempted to score, but missed home plate. His run counts as long as there is no appeal. However, R1 has also scored and did touch the plate. That act precludes R2 from returning.

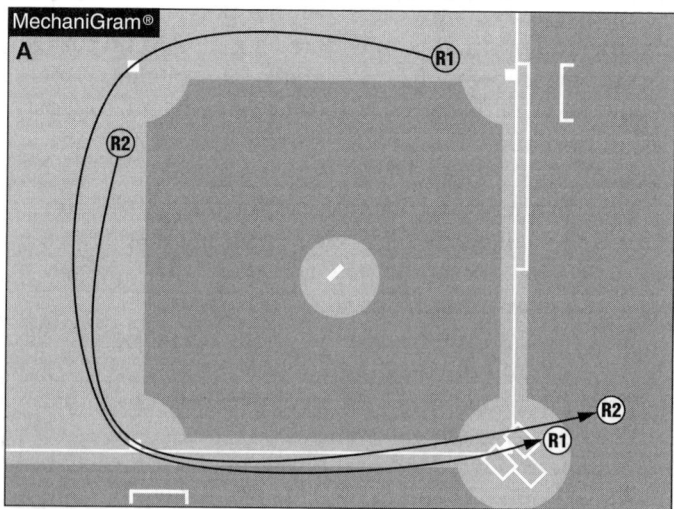

Once R1 touches the plate, R2 may not return to touch the missed base.

So even if R2 were to return to touch the plate, the defense could still properly appeal that R2 missed home and have that run removed from the board.

TIPS AND TECHNIQUES

In crew of two, the plate umpire has primary responsibility when R3 tags up and attempts to score on a fly ball that is caught. Because that play will happen before any others, such as the actual action at home plate, it should be the plate umpire's priority.

The plate umpire should move into a position to put the runner on third on an almost direct line between himself and the fielder making the catch. That requires minimal movement for a fly ball hit to the left side of the field and rather significant movement for balls hit to right field.

MechaniGram B shows the batter hitting a ball to left field with a runner on third. The plate umpire should move to his left, just outside of the dirt circle and be in a position to have both the catch and the runner tagging up in his field of vision. Once he has seen the tag, the plate umpire can move into position for a play at the plate.

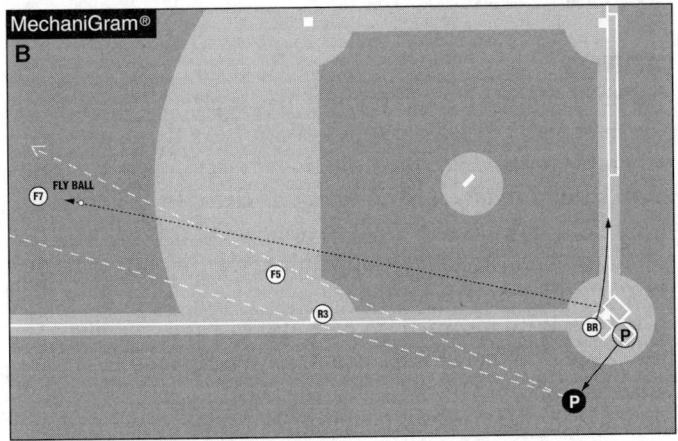

By moving out from behind the plate, the plate umpire can view the catch and the runner tagging at third.

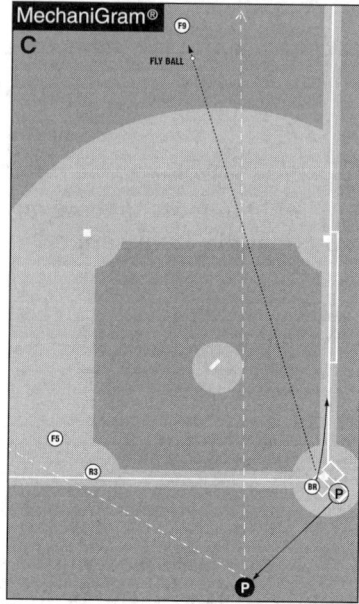

MechaniGram®
C
FLY BALL

A wider view is needed to observe a fly ball to right and the runner tagging at third.

MechaniGram C shows where the umpire should be on a fly ball hit to right field. Notice that he moves farther away from home plate and opens up a wider field of vision. It may not be possible to see both without a slight glance at the runner once the ball is caught.

In all cases, if there is an appeal, that call belongs to the plate umpire. Having the field of vision as open as possible adds believability to any appeal call, as opposed to camping out in the dirt circle. Hustle to get into position and there will be fewer arguments on the close calls.

CASEPLAYS

Play 1: With a runner on first, B1 singles. R1 advances toward third, but fails to touch second. As R1 nears third, the ball is returned to the infield and F6, holding the ball, kicks second in anger. **Ruling 1:** The defense has done nothing to indicate its intent to appeal the infraction, thus the umpire will make no call. Unless the defense appeals properly, R1 remains at third.

Play 2: With a runner on first and one out, B1 hits a line drive into the gap. R1 was stealing on the pitch. The ball is caught and R1 attempts to return to first. The ball is returned to first before R1 arrives, but he is not tagged. **Ruling 2:** R1 need not be tagged for the double play. The play situation and R1's attempt to return to first is an act that unmistakably indicates an appeal.

Play 3: With R1 on first, B1 hits a single and R1 advances to third. However, R1 misses second. F1 has the ball on the mound when F4's request for time is granted. F1 then tosses the ball to F4, who tags the base and appeals. **Ruling 3:** In NFHS, R1 is declared out; that is a legal appeal. In NCAA, the runner is not out yet. The ball must be live for a proper appeal to be made. A proper appeal can be made after the ball becomes live.

Play 4: With R3 on third base, B1 flies to left field. R3 tags, but leaves and scores before the ball is touched by F8. After the first pitch to B2, the defensive team appeals the illegal tag up. **Ruling 4:** The run counts. No appeal can be upheld after a pitch has been made.

Play 5: With R2 on second, B1 hits a single and R2 scores. The defense announces it will appeal that R2 missed third. With a live ball the pitcher prepares to make his appeal when B1, who has stopped at first, breaks for second. F1's throw is (a) in time to retire B1, or (b) not in time. **Ruling 5:** The appeal opportunity is not lost because the offense initiated a play. The defense is allowed to make a play on B1 without losing its appeal privilege.

Play 6: R2 scores on B1's single. The defense announces it will appeal that R2 missed third. As the pitcher toes the rubber in the set position, he sees that B1 has taken a long lead at first. F1's pickoff move, though, is not in time. F3 then fires to F5, who appeals R2. **Ruling 6:** It is too late to appeal. The play initiated by F1 canceled any potential appeal.

Play 7: F1's throw to F3 to appeal B2's failure to touch first base is thrown into dead-ball territory. **Ruling 7:** Under NFHS rules, an appeal may be made while the ball is dead; therefore there is no reason to make a live-ball appeal. If, however, such an appeal were made, a throw into dead-ball territory would not cancel the appeal. In NCAA, a throw into dead-ball territory cancels the appeal.

Play 8: With R1 on first, R2 on second and two out, B1 triples, scoring both runners. R1, however, misses third base. F5 informs the plate umpire that his pitcher is going to appeal. On the appeal attempt at third, the ball is thrown away and rolls toward the stands. B1, who is standing on third, scores easily. F5 retrieves the ball and tags third, officially appealing the missed base. **Ruling 8:** In NFHS, F5's statement could constitute an appeal. If the umpire recognizes the attempt and calls time, the dead-ball appeal can be granted. In NCAA, both runs count. The appeal is invalidated.

Play 9: With the bases loaded, B1 hits a looping fly ball. F7 makes a spectacular catch for the first out. He fires the ball to second for out number two on R2, who failed to tag up. The triple play is completed when F4 fires to first for the third out on R1, who also failed to tag up. R3 scored before the out at first, but he also never retouched. **Ruling 9:** Even though R3 did not properly retouch, his run counts since the defensive team did not properly appeal. It is a time play. Even though the inning has ended, the defense may appeal R3 before it leaves the field. That fourth out will cancel the run.

Play 10: With a runner on first and no outs, B1 hits a ball deep down the right-field line. R1, who was running on the pitch, is standing on third base when the ball is ruled foul. R1 then trots across the diamond back to first base. **Ruling 10:** R1 need only return to first. He does not need to retouch second. There is no appeal for not retouching as long as the runner is in the vicinity of the base. Once the ball is put in play, R1 is legally on first base even if he did not retouch any bases. The ball should never be put into play until all runners have returned to their original bases.

Play 11: R3 is on third with one out. B4 hits a fly ball to center field. In an attempt to gain speed, R3 backs up behind third base and tries to time it so that he tags up at third at the same time that F8 makes the catch. **Ruling 11:** That is not a legal move by R3. Under NFHS rules, the runner is called out immediately (the ball is delayed dead). Under NCAA rules, the runner is out only if the defense makes a proper appeal.

Play 12: With R2 on second and two outs, B5 hits a single to right field. R2 touches third and heads home. R2 crosses but does not touch home just in advance of B5 being retired for the third out at second base. The defense makes no appeal. **Ruling 12:** A runner is considered legally advanced to a base when he has passed it, even if he hasn't touched it. By not touching a base, the runner has left himself subject to being called out on appeal. Until such appeal is made, however, the runner is assumed to have touched the base and the run would score, even though a key provision for scoring a run (legally touching home plate) has not been met.

Play 13: With R2 on second and two outs, B5 hits a single to right field. R2 touches third and heads home. R2 crosses but does not touch home just in advance of B5 being retired for the third out at second base. The defense properly appeals the missed base. **Ruling 13:** A fourth out appeal allows the defense the opportunity to appeal the missed base and prevent the run from scoring even though the end of the inning (three outs) had already occurred. If the defense properly appeals, the run would not count.

Play 14: With R2 on second and two outs, B5 hits a single to right field. R2 touches third and heads home. R2 crosses but does not touch home just in advance of B5 being retired for the third out at second base. Immediately after the third out, R2 immediately returns and touches home. The defense makes no appeal. **Ruling 14:** That specific play is not covered in any rulebook or official casebook. If the runner had not returned to touch home, the play would be identical to play 12, and the run would score. The question is then what impact on the play does R2's return to the plate have.

The argument in disallowing the run is that the runner failed to touch home plate before the third out occurred. By returning, he is, in effect, completing his obligation to legally touch the plate. And since he failed

to legally touch until after the third out, his run cannot count.

The argument for counting the run is that the runner should not be penalized for returning to the plate. His actions before the third out would clearly have resulted in a run scoring had he made no attempt to retouch the plate. Rather than directly penalizing the runner, that retouch should only serve as a reminder to the defense (if observed) that something is wrong with the play.

Seeing the confusion, *Referee* asked the rules editors for the NFHS and NCAA and received interpretations. Both rules editors said that the run would score absent an appeal. While not using the same language, they concluded that once the third out is made, the only action that can happen to prolong an inning is a "fourth out" appeal. That does not preclude any serious rules infractions, such as malicious contact, from being enforced. Only routine offensive action ends with the third out.

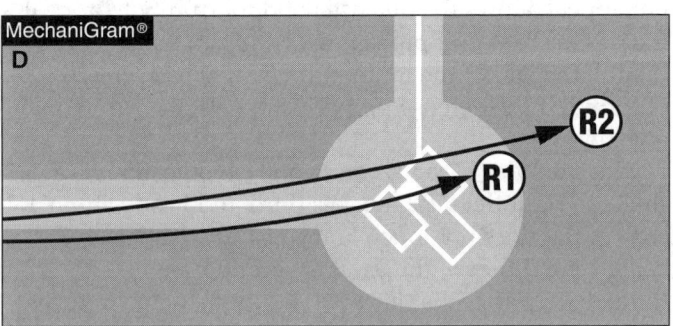

Unless the defense properly appeals, R2's run counts despite the fact R2 missed the plate.

Play 15: As seen in the MechaniGram D, R2, who started on second base, crosses but doesn't touch home plate. R1, who started on first, then touches the plate and scores. **Ruling 15:** If the defense properly appeals, R2 is out. Since that was the third out, R1's run is disallowed. Once a following runner has scored, it's not permissible for a runner to touch a missed base.

Play 16: With the bases loaded and two out, B1 hits a home run. On appeal, R1 is called out for missing third base. **Ruling 16:** Two runs score. A run is not scored if a runner advances to home during action in which the third out is made by a preceding runner who is declared out for missing a base.

Play 16: With the bases loaded and two out, B5 hits a home run. On appeal, R1 is called out for missing second base. **Ruling 16:** No runs score. Since R1 was forced to second base and did not successfully reach it, no runs can score.

Play 18: R1 is on first when B2 smacks a hit to the gap in left-center. R1 misses second base on his way to third base. F8 throws to F6, whose relay goes into dead-ball territory before R1 reaches third. Can R1 go back and touch second? Does the award for the throw supersede the missed base? Does the defense have to appeal in order to get the out on R1? **Ruling 18:** The award for the throw does not supersede the missed base. R1 is required to go back and touch second before proceeding on the award. If he does not retouch second, the defense may appeal to get the out on R1.

Play 19: With R2 on second, B7 gets a base hit. The throw from left field is not handled properly by the catcher and he fails to tag R2. However, R2 slid around the plate and did not touch it. He celebrates that he "scored" and heads into the dugout. **Ruling 19:** The umpire cannot make any signal since the runner is neither safe nor out. If the ball remains live, the defense must tag the plate and make an appeal. If the ball is declared dead, the ball must be returned to the pitcher and once it is made live, the pitcher must step off and appeal. In NFHS only, the coach or any player can make a dead-ball appeal. The plate umpire must be careful not to tip off the defense by his actions. If the defense does not appeal, the run counts. Under no circumstance can R2 return to touch home once he has entered the dugout.

CHAPTER 2

BALKS

A balk is an illegal act by a pitcher with a runner or runners on base. The result of a balk is that all runners get to advance one base.

That definition from the *Official Baseball Rules* is repeated in the NCAA and NFHS rulebooks as well.

Nowhere in the two-sentence definition nor in the later rules that explain what those illegal acts are does the word "deception" appear. Yet go to any game and uninformed players, coaches and fans will be yelling for a balk to be called because the pitcher "deceived" the runner.

If there were time to educate the masses, an umpire could explain that deceiving the batter and the runners is the primary job of a pitcher. If a runner knew when a pickoff throw was (or was not) coming, he could better time his advance to the next base. At the same time, if a batter knows the next pitch is going to be a curve ball,

he can tee off and have a greater chance of getting a base hit.

So if deception isn't a balk, then what is? There are actually a lot of illegal acts by a pitcher that can be ruled a balk. The key, however, lies in the definition. There must be a runner or runners on base. Without that, you may have an illegal pitch, but you definitely do not have a balk.

Feinting toward the batter or first base. According to *The Official Rules of Baseball Illustrated*, feinting toward the batter was never intended to prevent a batter from swinging when a pitch wasn't actually thrown. Instead, it was written to prevent the pitcher from tricking the runner to leave early while the pitcher still has the ball.

Failing to step directly toward a base with the non-pivot foot when throwing or feinting toward that base. According to the same book, before 1899, pitchers were free to do just about anything they wanted in an attempt to pick off runners. Not only could they fake throws to first, they could also twitch their pitching shoulders, swing their legs in any number of directions and make any other number of moves which are now illegal under the current balk rules.

Dropping the ball (even if accidental) when the ball does not cross a foul line. If the pitcher is on the rubber and drops the ball, it is a balk if it does not cross (or is prevented from crossing) the foul line. If the ball crosses the foul line, it is treated like a pitch and is called a ball.

Failing to pitch to the batter in a continuous motion immediately after any movement of any part of the body that he habitually uses in his delivery. More commonly referred to as a "start-and-stop" balk, it occurs when the pitcher does just that. He has made a motion that clearly indicates he is going to pitch or make a pickoff throw.

A common instance of a move that has been ruled legal in NCAA, but illegal in NFHS play involves the

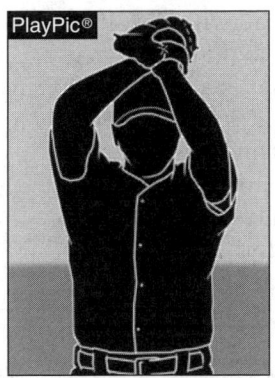
Pausing at the top of the windup is a balk in NFHS.

pitcher stopping in the middle of his windup. The pitcher starts his pitching motion and, while his hands are over his head and his free foot is behind the rubber, comes to a complete pause (see PlayPic). No matter how brief, that pause violates the rule and should be called a balk at the NFHS level.

Taking a hand off the ball while in the set position. Once the pitcher comes to his set position, with his hand on the ball in the glove, he may not remove his hand without first stepping off the rubber.

Throwing or feinting to an unoccupied base. The pitcher is not required to throw to second or third in order to keep a runner close. But if the pitcher inadvertently throws or feints to one of those bases when it isn't occupied, then it is a balk.

The exception to that rule is that a pitcher may throw to those bases for the purpose of completing an appeal play or if a play is imminent. For example, if R2 breaks from second early, the pitcher can throw to third, which is unoccupied, for the purpose of completing a play. That would be legal.

Failing to pitch to the batter when the entire non-pivot foot passes behind the back edge of the pitcher's plate (except when legally feinting or throwing to second base). A pitcher is committed to deliver a pitch once the free foot crosses behind the back edge of the pitcher's plate. If, at that point, he throws to first (left-handed pitcher) or third (right-handed pitcher), he has committed a balk.

Making an illegal pitch. A pitcher is not permitted to apply a foreign substance to the ball, spit on the ball or glove, rub the ball on his glove, clothing or person if it

defaces the ball or to discolor the ball with dirt. If he does any of those things, the ball should be declared dead. If it is not, and the pitcher makes a pitch, that pitch is illegal. With no runners on, the pitch is automatically a ball. If there is a runner or runners on base, it is a balk.

Failing to stop while in the set position. That is possibly the most common balk called. When a pitcher "comes set," he must completely stop, and such stop must be discernable. Because of that last word, the physics definition of a change of direction including a stop is not acceptable. The umpire must be able to tell that a pitcher has completely stopped.

A fairly new technique used by pitchers to gain an advantage involves coming to a complete and discernable stop with the hands, but starting the legs in motion at the same time. Both NFHS and NCAA rules now define a complete stop to mean all parts of the body.

NFHS PENALTIES

Before 1954 in MLB, when a balk was called, the ball was immediately dead and nothing else that happened mattered.

That rule remains the case in NFHS play. Even if a pitch is delivered and hit for an apparent home run, the balk call kills the play. Each runner advances one base and the batter remains at the plate with the same count as before the balk.

NCAA PENALTIES

The NCAA rules now mimic the pro rules, which do not immediately kill the play upon a balk.

A balk should be called and the ball declared dead if the pitcher does not immediately deliver the ball home (on a pitch) or to a base (on a pickoff attempt). If the pitcher does deliver the ball, play is allowed to continue until the pitch ends, is batted into play or a pickoff throw is caught.

That rule permits the offense to take advantage of a defensive miscue or bad pitch and gain more bases than just the balk would permit. If a pitch or pickoff throw is caught, the play should be stopped at that point. If the pitch or throw is wild or the ball is put into play, play should remain live until such time as action has stopped or it is apparent that the provisions of the balk penalty will not be met.

If the batter puts the ball into play, he and all runners must advance one base in order for the balk to be ignored. There are no offensive options.

Consider each of the potential happenings after a balk is called on the following plays under NCAA rules. In each case, unless otherwise stated, R1 is the only runner and he is on first.

Play 1: F1's pitch is caught without the batter putting it into play. **Ruling 1:** Time is called when the pitch is caught. The balk is enforced. R1 is awarded second base.

Play 2: F1's pitch is wild. **Ruling 2:** Time is not called until R1 has stopped. R1 is permitted to advance at his own risk beyond the awarded base. As long as R1 reaches second base, the balk is ignored.

Play 3: F1's pitch is wild, but R1 is thrown out at second. **Ruling 3:** Time is called when it is apparent R1 will not advance safely to second. Since R1 did not advance past the awarded base, the balk must be enforced and R1 is awarded second.

Play 4: F1's pickoff throw to first is caught as R1 is stealing second. **Ruling 4:** As soon as the pickoff throw is caught, time should be called and the balk enforced. Even if F3 throws the ball into the outfield and R1 could advance farther, the pickoff throw ended when it was caught and the balk is enforced.

Play 5: F1's pickoff throw goes into foul territory down the right-field line. **Ruling 5:** Play is permitted to continue. If the fielder who retrieves the ball subsequently throws wild, that is part of the same play and R1 is free to continue to run.

Play 6: Continue Play 5 and R1 is thrown out at third or home. **Ruling 6:** R1 is only protected to the awarded base (second). Since he was thrown out beyond that point, the out stands.

Play 7: B4 gets a base hit, advancing R1. **Ruling 7:** Since B4 and R1 both advanced one base, the balk is ignored and the play stands.

Play 8: With R1 stealing, B5 hits a ground ball to F3. F3 is able to step on first base to retire B5, but R1 advances to second. **Ruling 8:** Since B5 put the ball into play and did not advance one base, play should be stopped as soon as F3 steps on first base. The balk penalties are enforced. R1 is advance to second and B5 is brought back to the plate.

Play 9: With R2 on second, B5 hits a fly ball to deep left field. The ball is caught for the first out, but R2 legally tags and scores on the play. **Ruling 9:** Play is stopped as soon as the ball is caught. R2 is awarded third and B5 is returned to the plate. The offensive head coach does not have the option of taking the out and the run.

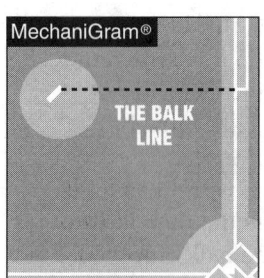

The balk line is an imaginary line.

STEPPING DIRECTLY TOWARD FIRST

For pickoffs at first (most common with left-handed pitchers), the pitcher must step directly and gain ground toward the base. "Directly" is usually construed to mean more toward first than to the plate. That translates to a 45-degree angle measured from the pivot foot toward first base. However, only the NCAA rulebook actually uses the 45-degree measurement in the rules covering that type of balk. Thus an imaginary line drawn from the center of the rubber to the mid-point between home and first becomes the "balk line" (MechaniGram). If the pitcher steps to the home plate side of that line when attempting a pickoff at first, he has balked.

Since the line won't be chalked or even drawn in the dirt, umpires must be more innovative in making the call. In the two-umpire system, the plate umpire has the best view and the criterion is whether or not the step of the non-pivot foot appeared as if a pitch were forthcoming.

Umpires must keep in mind, however, that where the foot lands is far from the only determination if the pitcher balked. If the pitcher brings his leg or body forward, starting a motion toward home, he has balked if he throws to first base, regardless of where his foot lands.

NFHS AND NCAA CASEPLAYS

Play 10: With R1 on first and R3 on third, F1, from the set position, fakes a throw to third base and then spins and throws toward first in an attempt to retire R1. Is that legal? **Ruling 10:** It can be, but F1 is under several restrictions. On the fake to third base, F1 must step more toward third base than to the plate. If he fails to do that or fails to gain ground toward third, it is an immediate balk and the ball is dead. Once he has completed the fake to third (with or without feinting a throw), the pitcher must break contact with the rubber before feinting or throwing to first under NCAA rules. NFHS rules do not require the pitcher to break contact with the rubber if he completes a legal pickoff throw to first. He must break contact with the rubber if he feints to first. If the pitcher's sole purpose is to deceive the runner at first base by making the move in one continuous motion without disengaging the rubber, a balk has occurred in all likelihood and should be called. Under both codes, if the pitcher disengages the rubber, he is allowed to fake toward first.

Play 11: With R1 on first and R2 on second, no outs and a full count to B3, the pitcher fails to stop as he throws the pitch. B3 swings, but the pitch is low and the catcher fails to catch it. The ball is deflected into the dugout. When the ball gets away from the catcher, B3 advances to first base successfully. **Ruling 11:** In NFHS, once a balk has been called, the ball is dead. R1 and R2 are each awarded a base and B3 remains at the plate with a full count. In NCAA, the net result is the same, although the reason is different. Because first base was occupied with fewer than two outs, B3 was ineligible to advance to first base on a dropped third strike. Once he is declared out, the provisions for ignoring a balk — all runners, including the batter, advancing one base safely — are not possible. Therefore the balk penalty must be enforced.

BALK RESPONSIBILITIES

The rules do not distinguish between which umpire is responsible for calling a balk. Therefore, umpires have concurrent jurisdiction and can call a pitcher for any of the reasons.

That being said, it is only practical that umpires "divide" the primary responsibility for the calling of balks.

Although the NFHS Umpires Manual does not assign particular responsibilities, the CCA manual does provide practical guidelines for who should be primarily responsible for each type of balk.

The plate umpire should concentrate on:
1. Left-handed pitchers stepping to home plate.
2. Left-handed pitchers coming to a complete stop.
3. Right-handed pitchers coming to a complete stop.
4. Right-handed pitchers stepping to the plate on the third to first move.
5. Right-handed pitchers gaining ground on the jump turn.
6. Right-handed pitchers closing their front shoulder before the jump turn.

The base umpire should concentrate on:
1. Left-handed pitchers coming to a complete stop.
2. Right-handed pitchers breaking their front knees before the jump turn.
3. Right-handed pitchers gaining ground on the jump turn.

MECHANICS

The NFHS umpires manual says that an umpire should "throw his hands up, which signifies the ball is dead, and call balk." Since all balks are immediately dead in NFHS, that mechanic is fine.

However, in NCAA (and all other levels of play that do not use NFHS rules), the umpire should not immediately kill the ball. The umpire should come out of his stance, point toward the pitcher and yell, "That's a balk." The umpire should then immediately get back into position to judge the pitch or play. When the pitch or play is over, the umpire should then call time and award bases as necessary.

NFHS

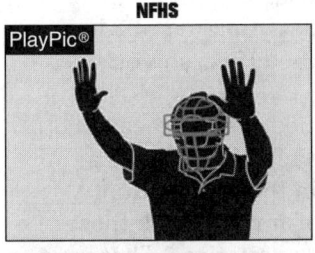

In NFHS, signal the ball dead (top), then call the balk.

NCAA

In NCAA, call the balk (top), but wait for action to end to call time.

Referee recommends that umpires follow the NCAA mechanic of pointing out the balk without immediately calling time. It is easier to let things happen, then kill the ball and explain why what just happened doesn't matter in NFHS than it is to explain why the umpire prematurely called time when the batter just roped an extra-base hit.

TIPS AND TRICKS

In every thorough pregame discussion that you've probably had, the phrase that has likely come up is, "If you see a balk, call it."

But the converse statement — "To call a balk, you have to see it" — is more appropriate.

To get balks correct, a number of umpires have methods they have used to aid themselves. Different umpires may have different "tricks," but all of the tricks involved the same basic premise. The umpire never wavers from watching the pitcher's actions.

Staying focused on the pitcher is a hard thing to do sometimes. Fielders or baserunners are asking you to move, you are giving your pre-play signals to your partner or just the fact that you are outside on a nice spring day instead of in the office, so you relax for just a split-second.

One veteran umpire explained that he measured a discernable stop by voicing to himself, "That's a stop." If the pitcher's "stop" in the set position lasted less time than it took for him to think those three words, then he balked it every time. That was his way of making sure that he was focused on the pitcher and his actions.

Another umpire, one that is now in professional baseball, uses a nearly opposite method of watching for balks throughout a pitcher's setup and delivery. Every pitch, he repeats the phrase, "That's OK," to himself while the pitcher has the potential to balk. "That's OK. That's OK. That's OK. That's OK. That's OK. ..."

As long as the pitcher stays within the rules, the umpire doesn't have to do anything. But as soon as something doesn't measure up to "That's OK," then he calls a balk.

Without ensuring that you are focused on watching the pitcher, you can't see the actions that might be illegal. So make certain you are watching for the balks and call them when you see them.

CHAP TER 3

BATTING OUT OF ORDER

It seems so simple: The players know their place in the batting order. The player who follows the teammate who batted last the previous inning is likely to lead off the next inning. But substitutions, ejections, injuries and plain old "brain cramps" sometimes cause confusion and lead to players batting out of order. It's as old as the game itself.

Perhaps the most unusual batting-out-of-order situation occurred May 19, 1913, when a manager pinch-hit for two men in the same inning.

With the New York Yankees trailing the St. Louis Browns, 3-1, in the top of the eighth inning, Yankee skipper Frank Chance, hoping to start a rally, put himself in as a pinch hitter in the ninth position for pitcher Ray Fisher. Chance promptly grounded out to shortstop Mike Balenti. However, the following hitters rallied.

They scored five runs and had runners on second and third with number eight hitter Claude Derrick scheduled to bat. But Chance erroneously came to bat one hitter early and drilled a two-run single to left. Leadoff man Bert Daniels then came to bat and grounded out for the second out of the inning with Chance advancing to second. Suddenly, Browns acting manager Lou Criger sprang out of the dugout. Criger excitedly complained to plate umpire George Hildenbrandt, "Chance batted for two different men this inning! You've got to call somebody out!"

Hildenbrandt remained calm and carefully examined his lineup card. The veteran umpire then informed Criger that although he was right about Chance, he had appealed batting out of order too late. Hildenbrandt explained that the first pitch to Daniels legalized Chance and the batting order was back in order and the results of his time at bat became legal. Criger was unhappy but became even unhappier when Hildenbrandt told him if he appealed batting out of order after Chance's hit, Derrick, the proper batter, would have been called out, the two-run single nullified and Chance would have then come to bat again as the proper batter. The Yankees ultimately won the game, 10-3.

TODAY'S RULES

In NFHS, the lineup card, presented by either the head coach or captain at the pregame meeting, shall include the name, shirt number, position and batting order of each starting player. The name and shirt number of each eligible substitute shall also be listed. Under NFHS rules, there is no penalty if a substitute is not listed, even though it is required. It is meant to speed up substitutions, not be a punitive rule.

In NCAA, the umpire-in-chief conducts the pregame meeting with the representatives of the opposing teams 10 minutes before the scheduled starting time. During the meeting, the umpire-in-chief receives from the home team and visiting team their respective batting orders, in duplicate. The umpire determines that the copies are identical, keeps one copy and gives the other copy to the opposing team's representative. At that point, the umpire is officially in charge of the game and the lineups are official.

The procedure for following the batting order is the same regardless of code. Each player of the team at bat shall become the batter and shall take his position within a batter's box, on either side of home plate, in the order in which his name appears on the lineup card as delivered to the umpire prior to the game. The order shall be followed during the entire game except that an entering substitute takes the replaced player's place in the batting order.

In NFHS, a designated hitter and the player for whom he is batting are locked into the batting order. No multiple substitutions may be made that will alter the batting rotation.

A batter is in proper order if he follows the player whose name precedes his in the lineup, even though the preceding batter may have batted out of order. An improper batter is considered to be at bat as soon as he is in the batter's box and the ball is live. When the improper batter's infraction is first discovered by either team, time may be requested and the improper batter replaced by the proper batter with the improper batter's ball and strike count still in effect, provided the infraction is detected before the improper batter is put out or becomes a base runner.

After the first inning, the first batter in each inning shall be the player whose name follows that of the last batter who completed his time at bat in the preceding inning.

A batter shall be called out, on appeal, when he fails to bat in his proper turn and another batter completes a time at bat in his place. Only the defensive team may appeal batting out of order after the batter has completed his time at bat. The offense cannot appeal after the plate appearance has been completed because there could be an unfair advantage gained. If the plate appearance is still in progress, there is no extra advantage to be gained.

When an improper batter becomes a runner or is put out and the defensive team appeals to the umpire before the first legal or illegal pitch, play or attempted play, intentional base on balls or before the infielders leave the diamond if a half-inning is ending, the umpire shall declare the proper batter out and return all runners to the base occupied at the time of the pitch.

When an improper batter becomes a runner or is put out and a legal pitch or illegal pitch has been delivered to the succeeding batter, or an intentional base on balls has occurred, or all infielders have left the diamond if a half inning is ending, and before an appeal is made, the improper batter becomes the proper batter and the results of his time at bat become legal.

When the proper batter is called out because he has failed to bat in turn, the next batter shall be the batter whose name follows that of the proper batter thus called out.

When an improper batter becomes a proper batter because no appeal is properly made, the next batter shall be the batter whose name follows that of such legalized improper batter. The instant an improper batter's actions are legalized, the batting order picks up with the name following that of the legalized improper batter. When several players bat out of order before discovery so that a player's time at bat occurs while he is a runner, that player remains on base, but he is not out as a batter.

In NCAA, if two or more substitute players of the defensive team enter the game simultaneously, the coach or a representative immediately shall designate to the umpire-in-chief the position of each in the team's batting order. If that is not done immediately, the umpire shall place them in the batting order. Also, when the designated hitter and the pitcher both enter on defense at the same time, the coach must designate the positions in the batting order of the new pitcher and the previous pitcher.

When batting out of order is discovered at the right time in NCAA rules, the proper batter is out and other runners are returned to the bases occupied at the time of the pitch. The improper batter, if on base, is removed from base and any outs made by ordinary play are canceled.

In NFHS, outs made by ordinary play stand after batting out of order is penalized except any out made by the improper batter is superseded by the out declared for batting out of order.

ADVANCES WHILE IMPROPER BATTER IS AT BAT

In both codes, runners who advance independent of an improper batter's actions are entitled to those advances. For example, if the runner advances because of a stolen base, wild pitch, passed ball or balk during the improper batter's plate appearance, he is entitled to keep that advancement.

Any advance made as a direct result of the improper batter's actions are not permitted.

TIPS AND TECHNIQUES

The late Nick Bremigan, former MLB umpire and umpire school instructor, devised a simplified batting-out-of-order system for umpires to follow. Essentially, Bremigan broke down the wordy rule into three courses of action for the umpire:

• **Batting out of order discovered too soon.** That happens when the defensive team appeals batting out of order while the wrong batter is still at bat. In that case there is no penalty. The proper batter is simply brought to the plate and assumes the improper batter's count.

• **Batting out of order discovered at the right time.** That occurs when batting out of order is appealed immediately after the improper batter completes his turn at bat and before the next pitch. In that case, the proper batter is declared out and the next batter is the batter who follows the player just called out.

• **Batting out of order discovered too late.** That happens when a batting-out-of-turn appeal is made following the first pitch to the next batter. That pitch legalizes the improper batter. In that situation, no one is called out and the proper batter is the player who follows the legalized improper batter in the order.

There are three keys to keep in mind: When a player bats out of turn, the proper batter (not the improper batter) is called out upon proper appeal; if the defense does not properly appeal, the improper batter is legalized and that establishes the order that is to follow; and the umpire need only concern himself with the last two players who have batted. No matter which player batted last, the batter immediately before him was legal, therefore the correct last batter will always be the name that follows that of the player who batted immediately before the last batter.

Although batting order foul-ups can occur any time, specific situations seem to be ripe for problems. They include but are not limited to situations in which a substitute enters (for strategic purposes or due to an ejection or injury), when the third out is made by a runner rather than the batter (such as an unsuccessful steal or a pickoff) and, in NFHS play, when a substituted player re-enters.

CASEPLAYS

Play 1: The scorekeeper, public-address announcer or a fan informs the umpire of a player batting out of order. **Ruling 1:** In NFHS, the umpire shall remain silent, unless the defense brings the infraction to his attention. In NCAA, the umpires, official scorer or public-address announcer shall not call attention to the improper batter. If that occurs, the umpire-in-chief shall warn the official scorer and/or the public-address announcer that on the next infraction the offending person will be removed from the position.

Play 2: With R1 on first, B2 is the next batter in the batting order, but B3 erroneously takes his place. The coach of the defensive team points out the situation after (a) a pitch to B3, (b) B3 singles, or (c) after a pitch has been delivered to B4. **Ruling 2:** In (a), there is no penalty. B2 takes the place of B3 at the plate and assumes the count. If R1 advanced through a steal or wild pitch while the incorrect batter was batting, it is a legal advance. In (b), B2 is declared out and B3 takes his regular turn at bat. R1 must return to first. In (d), it is too late to correct the error. B4 remains at bat.

Play 3: It is B3's turn to bat but B5 bats instead. B5 has a 1-1 count when the error is noticed. **Ruling 3:** Because the infraction was noticed before the improper batter was put out or became a runner, the error can be corrected without penalty. B3 will take B5's place and assume the 1-1 count.

Play 4: It is B1's turn to bat but B3 bats instead. Who bats after B3 if the problem is not corrected? **Ruling 4:** B4 would take his normal turn because he follows B3 in the order. B1 and B2 are skipped until their turns come up in the order again.

Play 5: It is B3's turn to bat but B5 bats instead. On the first pitch, B5 swings and misses and R1 steals second. Either team then notices B3 is supposed to be at bat. Must R1 return to first? **Ruling 5:** R1's advance is legal. B3 takes his place at bat and assumes the 0-1 count.

Play 6: R2 is on second and R1 on first with no outs. It is B3's turn to bat but B4 erroneously bats and hits a ground ball to F5. F5 steps on third to force out R2 and fires to F4 at second to force out R1. B4 is safe at first. The defensive team then appeals batting out of order. **Ruling 6:** In NCAA B3, the batter who should have batted, is declared out. The outs on R2 and R1 are nullified and they are returned to their original bases. B4 is removed from base and returns to the plate as the proper batter. In NFHS, it's a triple play. The outs on R2 and R1 stand and B3 is declared out for failing to bat in proper order. B4 will lead off the next inning.

    Play 7: The batting order is Abel, Baker, Charles, Daniel, Edward, Frank, etc. It is Abel's turn to bat, but Charles bats and hits a double. Abel then comes to bat and strikes out. Baker follows and also strikes out. It is now Charles's turn to bat, but Charles is on second base. **Ruling 7:** Charles is left on second base, skipped over in the batting order and the proper batter is Daniels.

    Play 8: B8 is hitting in the position where B7 should be. R1 is on first base and successfully steals second base. R1 then advances to third on a throwing error by the catcher. B8 hits a fly ball to center field that scores the runner. The defense then appeals batting out of order. **Ruling 8:** B7 is ruled out because he was the proper batter and did not bat in turn. The runner is returned to third. He is not allowed to keep the advance on the sacrifice fly, but is entitled to the advances because of the stolen base and throwing error. B8 returns to the plate as the proper batter.

CHAP TER 4

Force-Play Slide Rule

Crusty old Ty Cobb likely rolled over in his grave when he heard that a rule was instituted to reduce contact by runners on force plays. Cobb, the epitome of the player who would do whatever was necessary to win a game, was famous for barreling into second base to upset the pivot on a double play.

Force plays are prime situations for contact. A force play is one in which a runner legally loses his right to occupy a base by reason of the batter becoming a runner.

One can argue that a bit of "good ol' time baseball" died when the NFHS and NCAA instituted the force-play slide rule. But the fact that countless injuries are prevented because of the rule more than overcomes any feelings of nostalgia.

On any force play at any base, a runner who slides must slide directly to the base with his entire body. He can legally slide either head-first or butt-down as long as he goes directly to the base. College players are permitted to slide directly through the bag or to pop up at the bag legally. NFHS rules permit neither act if they interfere with the fielder.

Contact with a fielder is legal if the runner legally slides directly toward a base and is sliding when a throw brings the fielder between bases to make a play. That is depicted in PlayPic A. A sliding runner is also exempted if he contacts a fielder who is on or over the base. NCAA also permits contact directly behind the bag.

PlayPic®

A

If the throw brings the fielder into the path of a runner's legal slide, there is no violation.

When a runner is guilty of interference under the force-play slide rule, he is out and the umpire will also call the out batter-runner for his teammate's interference. All other runners return to the base occupied at the time of the pitch.

A play on the batter-runner at first base can never be a force play and, although it has almost all the attributes of a force play and can be thought of as such for most purposes, the force-play slide rule never applies at first base.

Play 1: R1 is on first with no outs. B1 smashes a one-hopper to F6, whose flip to F4 at second retires R1. However, F4's bullet relay to first strikes R1, who is in the baseline about halfway to second. **Ruling 1:** In NFHS, the runner is not expected to slide halfway between first and second. As long as he doesn't intentionally interfere, the play stands and the ball remains live. NCAA rules do not make an exception based on the runner's position. He must slide or get out of the way of the throw. That is interference. B1 is out because of R1's actions.

ILLEGAL SLIDES

An illegal slide results in the runner being called out for interference.

Any illegal slide results in an interference call. Illegal slides include one with the runner's leg positioned higher than the fielder's knee (PlayPic B) or a "barrel roll" into the base. Interference is also called when a runner makes illegal contact with a fielder, runs or slides toward a fielder to disrupt the fielder's play or attempted play or alter his pattern of play, or slides toward or contacts a fielder even if the fielder makes no attempt to throw to complete a play.

The runner may not use a rolling or cross-body block; have a leg raised above the fielder's knee when in a standing position; or slash, or kick the fielder with either leg, or otherwise attempt to injure him. NFHS rules also prohibit pop-up slides or going beyond the base and either making contact with or altering the play of the fielder.

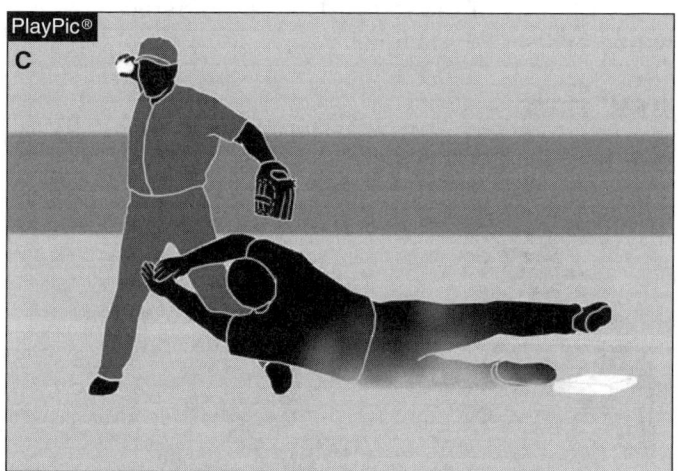

Failing to slide directly into the base is ruled an illegal slide.

When a runner is forced, a legal slide is not good enough. The runner must slide directly to the base. "Directly" means the runner's entire body (feet, legs, trunk and arms) must stay in a straight line between the bases. Of course, the runner is not required to slide, but may run away from the fielder.

The runner's slide in PlayPic C is illegal in both NFHS and NCAA play because the runner did not slide directly into the bag.

NFHS rules do not require a runner to slide, but when they slide, it must be legal. The slide is illegal since on a force play, the runner did not slide on the ground and in a direct line between the two bases.

In NCAA, on a force play, the runner must slide on the ground before the base and in a direct line between the two bases. However, if he slides or runs away from the fielder to avoid making contact, he is still legal. The NCAA rulebook shows a diagram of the legal sliding area. The runner can slide to, on top of or through the bag as long as it's in a direct line between the two bases.

Play 2: With R1 on first, B1 grounds to F6, who flips to F4 at second. R1 slides directly over and through the bag where F4 is standing and (a) contacts, or (b) does not contact F4. **Ruling 2:** In NFHS, that results in a double play in either case because the slide was not direct into the bag. It does not matter whether the non-direct slide resulted in contact or altered the play. If the runner does not slide directly to the base, it is interference and a double play unless the slide was away from the fielder. If the slide is toward the fielder, contact is not a factor. In NCAA, sliding directly beyond the bag is legal.

Play 3: With R1 on first, B1 grounds to F6, who flips to F4 at second. R1 pops up into F4 (a) before, or (b) after F4 drops the ball. **Ruling 3:** In NFHS, that results in a double play in either case because of the illegal slide on a force play. It does not matter whether the slide caused the dropped ball, nor does it matter whether R1 would have been safe or out at second. In NCAA, the pop up slide at the bag is legal.

Play 4: With R1 on first, B1 grounds to F6, who flips to F4 at second. R1 pops up but he otherwise slides directly into the base. He does not make contact or alter the play. **Ruling 4:** Legal. That type of illegal slide is interference only if there is contact or the play is altered.

Play 5: With R1 on first, B1 grounds to F6, who flips to F4 at second. R1 slides late and goes directly into the base almost standing. He contacts F4's arm as F4 is throwing to first. **Ruling 5:** That is a double play because R1 didn't slide and made contact.

MECHANICS

With a runner on first only and fewer than two outs, a ground ball in the infield can lead to a double play. While the base umpire is responsible for both halves of the double play, the plate umpire also has a job to do.

Because the base umpire must turn away from second to focus on the back half of the double play, the plate umpire has primary responsibility on any following action at second base.

Once a ground ball has been hit, the plate umpire needs to move out toward the left side of the mound

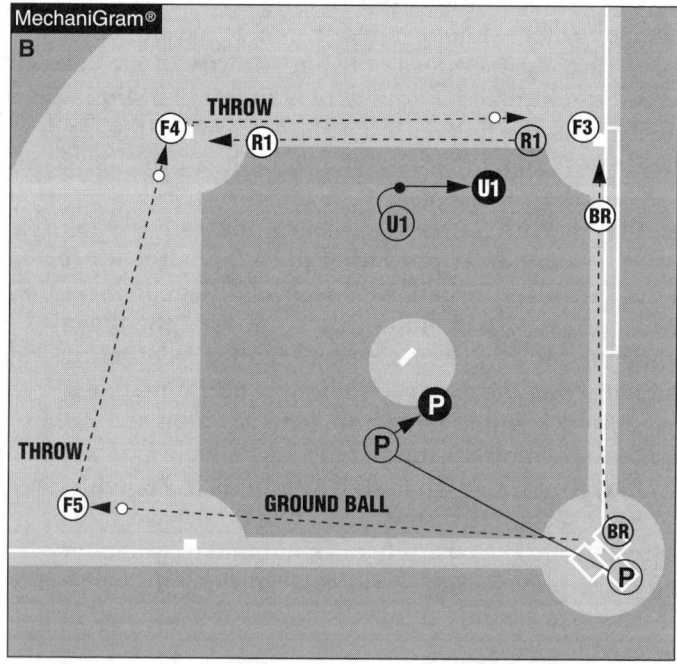

Because the base umpire must pivot to make the call at first, the plate umpire has to move to watch action by the runner at second base.

(MechaniGram B) in order to observe the action at second base. If there is an illegal slide, the plate umpire should immediately call time and penalize the interference.

Because the plate umpire is focused on second base, he usually cannot provide any assistance on the play at first in case of a pulled foot or swipe tag. The base umpire must be aware of that and get into the best position possible to judge that play. Sometimes, but not often, the action at second base never materializes and the plate umpire can turn and attempt to help.

CHAP TER 5

Hit by Pitch

Hall of Famer Don Drysdale was one of the most feared pitchers in the history of baseball. He had uncanny command of his blazing fastball and used it to strike out 2,486 batters in his 14-year career. But Drysdale let it be known he would have no compunction about hitting a batter who crowded the plate or broke one of baseball's other unwritten rules of conduct.

Drysdale hit 154 batters (he led the NL in hit batters five times, including four seasons in a row) and brushed back hundreds of others. Legend has it one batter stepped up to the plate and began to dig a deep hole for his back foot. The catcher interrupted the batter's excavation efforts. "You do realize who's pitching today, don't you?" The batter looked up, saw a scowling Drysdale on the mound and quickly began to fill in the hole.

Hit batters are a fairly common occurrence in modern baseball. They occur because pitchers temporarily lose command of their control, because a batter crowds the plate or because a pitcher attempts to jam the hitter and pitches the ball too far inside.

THE RULES

The ball is dead any time a pitch hits the batter. If the batter is hit by a pitch he offers at or a pitch in the strike zone touches him, he is not awarded first base (PlayPic A). In those cases, just add a strike to the batter's count. Remember, the ball is dead.

A batter is not awarded first base if he is hit by the pitch but the pitch is ruled a called or swinging strike.

The batter must try to avoid being struck by the pitch. No batter is allowed to obtain first by moving into the pitch (PlayPic B). However, if the batter freezes on a pitch at him (NCAA rules specify the pitch must be

It is illegal for a batter to move in such a way that allows him to be hit by a pitch.

clearly inside the vertical lines of the batter's box) and consequently makes no attempt to avoid the pitch, he is awarded first base. That situation is managed differently than the batter who obviously allows the ball to strike him by making no attempt to avoid the pitch. In the latter situation, add a ball or strike to the batter's count but do not award him first base.

It is hoped that umpires — unlike the average coach, fan, commentator and even player — know that the hands are not part of the bat. If a pitch hits a batter's hand before hitting the bat and the batter did not swing, it is a hit batter. If the batter swung at the pitch — including a checked swing rung up as a swing — it is simply a swinging strike. If the batter checks his swing, the ruling is no swing and he takes his base.

The hit batter rule has a colorful (black and blue?) history. In 1884, the American Association adopted a

rule for awarding the batter first base for being struck by a pitch. The rule was instituted because John Schappert, while pitching for St. Louis in 1882, threw at so many hitters. In 1887, the Official Baseball Rules granted a hitter, in legal batting position, first base if a pitch touched him or his clothing. Essentially, that is the current rule. However, NFHS rules are unique in stating the batter's uniform must be reasonably well-fitted for the clothing aspect of the rule to be enforced.

From 1892-96, a batter was not awarded first if a pitch struck him on his hand or forearm, though the ball was declared dead. That may be why many people now mistakenly believe the batter's hands are considered part of the bat. In 1897 it was decided to give the batter first if a pitch struck any part of his body, including his hands or forearms.

It was not until 1957 that the rule addressed a batter being hit by a strike. Minnie Minoso of the White Sox had a major bearing on that addendum to the rule. Minoso, who crowded the plate, was frequently hit by pitches near the strike zone. Minnie was denied first base several times in his career after being struck by a pitch in the strike zone.

It is possible that a pitch can strike both the batter's hand and the bat. In that situation, it is recommended that you grant the batter first base. Since the hand was on top of the bat, consider the hand was hit first.

An umpire should never award the batter first if he intentionally moves into a pitch and gets hit. Though the batter was "plunked," add a ball to his count when he deliberately moves into a pitch and contacts the ball.

There is precedent for an umpire to deny a batter first because the pitch was a strike. During a game in the 1996 season, the Dodgers' Brett Butler suffered a broken left hand but went to the clubhouse rather than first base. The injury occurred with one out and no one on in the fourth inning when Butler tried to bunt for a base hit. Right-hander Giovanni Carrara's inside pitch struck Butler's hand as he turned to drag-bunt the ball.

The Associated Press erroneously reported that plate umpire Bill Hohn ruled the pitch a foul ball because Butler's hand was on the bat when it was struck. Hohn actually ruled that Butler attempted to bunt the pitch that hit him. Hohn correctly called an immediate dead ball when Butler was struck. Because Butler attempted to strike at the pitch that contacted him, a strike was added to his count and he was not awarded first base. Since Butler had to leave the game, Wayne Kirby was allowed to come to bat and assume Butler's count. Had the pitch to Butler been strike three, he would have been declared out.

Similarly, umpires have denied batters first base because their actions caused them to be hit by a pitch. Former AL umpire Hank Soar refused to let Nellie Fox of the White Sox go to first after being hit in June 1956. Fox intentionally turned his butt into a slow curve thrown by Baltimore Oriole lefthander Johnny Schmitz. Two pitches later, Fox was hit again. That time Soar allowed Fox to go to first base.

In 1968, NL arbiter Harry Wendelstedt had a hand in Don Drysdale's breaking of Walter Johnson's consecutive scoreless innings streak (the record is now held by Orel Hershiser). The San Francisco Giants loaded the bases in the ninth inning and Dick Dietz was at bat with a 2-2 count when he was nicked by an inside pitch. Wendlestedt ruled that Dietz did not try to get out of the way of the pitch and he was not awarded first base. Dietz then flied out and Drysdale's streak was extended.

In the early 1950s Casey Stengel offered $50 to any batter on the Yankees who "took one for the team." After getting hit twice in the same game, Hank Bauer went with his bruises to collect his money. However, the cunning Old Professor would only fork over a single $50 bill to his hustling outfielder. The next day when Bauer hit a home run, Stengel gave him the rest of his reward.

MECHANICS

When a pitch hits a batter, the plate umpire will declare the ball dead, then verbally award first base. It is dangerous to point to first base; if the batter checked his swing, the base umpire could interpret the pointing signal as a request from the plate umpire to rule on the checked swing.

If the pitch hits the batter but the pitch results in a called or swinging strike, the plate umpire declares the ball dead, then signals a strike. Some umpires point toward the plate and verbalize, "The batter does not get first." Another optional mechanic approved in some areas involves the plate umpire indicating what part of the batter's body the pitch hit. For instance, the umpire can tap his own elbow while verbalizing, "Got 'im on the elbow."

It is important to observe the batter's reaction. Not every batter reacts negatively to being hit by a pitch. But since too many players unschooled in the finer points of baseball become angry even when plunked by an 0-2 changeup, umpires need to work quickly and head off problems before they begin.

As the plate umpire, prepare for the worst — a batter charging the mound — every time a batter gets hit. After calling time and awarding first base, step quickly around the catcher and jog up the baseline with the batter for at least a few strides. Watch the batter and use your voice to ensure the batter remains calm and heads toward first. By positioning yourself between the batter and the pitcher, you can prevent most volatile situations.

Some batters may linger in the box and glare at the pitcher or begin a dialogue with the catcher. Others may move toward first base. But that doesn't mean commentary or even a charge toward the mound is beyond the realm of possibility. Moving between the catcher, the mound and the batter puts the umpire in position to move quickly to quell a disturbance or at least let players know he's paying attention.

TIPS AND TECHNIQUES

A hit batter is one of those instances in which things can occur so quickly that it can be easy not to see or digest what happened. You can also get blocked out by the catcher. To avoid those problems, veteran NCAA umpire Jon Bible suggests hesitating a second or two and doing nothing. If he does that, Bible, says, "I'll get enough clues to piece together the proper answer. That is not enough of a hesitation, moreover, to cause coaches and fans to throw that old bromide, 'Make up your mind!' in your face. Because everyone's attention is focused on what happened with the batter, they really don't notice that you are not making an instantaneous decision."

One clue on which the umpire can rely is sound. There is a distinct, mushy "splat" sound when a pitch hits a hand, even gloved, compared to the sound when a ball hits a bat.

The second thing is the batter's reaction. Sure, it's possible to get deked every once in a great while, but in youth ball, high school and even college, few batters are mentally quick enough to be able to instantly turn in an Academy Award performance when the ball really hit the bat first. When his first reaction is to jump up and down, grab his hand, grimace, yell, cry, etc., you will almost certainly conclude that he got hit and award him first base. On the other hand, if the batter hesitates for a couple of seconds and then begins having a mild seizure, you probably should not buy what he's selling.

"The problem often is that we get too quick," Bible says. The pitch comes in, the batter starts his swing and something hits something. An umpire will immediately yell, 'Foul ball,' only to look up and see the batter writhing in pain. "Then to cover up, we go into some spiel about the pitch hitting the bat first and then the hand," Bible says. "No way my eyesight is that good, and I doubt yours is either. It's a cock and bull story,

pure and simple, that we would most likely not have had to concoct if we had waited to let the circumstances tell us what happened. I don't mean 10 seconds; just a second or two. That will be enough for the sound and the batter's reaction to tell you what happened. Timing is everything in that instance, just as it is in calling pitches."

Detecting some types of hit-batter situations is difficult because of the basic position in which we set up behind the plate. It puts us at a bad angle to detect if a pitch nicked the batter. Many basketball officials are familiar with the concept of being straight-lined from the play, which means that a player's body blocks the view of what you need to see to make a 100 percent accurate call. Basketball officials are taught to move to the space between the defense and offense to prevent being blocked out of the play. That is not practical for baseball umpires, however, because the position that you need to call balls and strikes can be a terrible position from which to see if the batter was nicked with a pitch. But you are still obligated to make a call.

The police use two types of evidence to determine if a person committed a crime: direct evidence and circumstantial evidence. Direct evidence in a hit-batter situation is an umpire seeing or hearing the batter getting hit. If you see the batter get hit, it's usually an easy call and you award the batter first.

But what if you didn't see the ball hit the batter? Without direct evidence, you might have to rely on circumstantial evidence. A smoking gun near a dead body with fingerprints all over it is a good example of circumstantial evidence. In hit-batter situations, if you don't see the ball hit the batter, you too should use circumstantial evidence to make your decision.

Using circumstantial evidence involves accepting the reality that in a small percentage of instances you will be wrong. Play the percentages of what probably happened, mix in some common sense and you can become quite proficient at handling these situations.

What are some of the criteria or types of circumstantial evidence you can use?

1. The batter's reaction. If the batter grimaces in pain immediately after the ball passes him, there is a good chance he was hit. Most first reactions are honest, and you can safely send the batter down to first. Sure, once in a while a batter will try to fool you, but umpiring involves compromise.

2. Sound. Sometimes you hear a sound as the ball passes the batter. If you hear a sound other than the ball hitting or nicking the catcher's glove or the bat, the batter was probably hit.

3. Location of the ball. If you have a fastball down the middle of the batter's box and you are in doubt as to whether or not the pitch got a piece of the batter, give the benefit of the doubt to the batter. Why? A pitched ball belongs around the plate, not over the middle of the batter's box.

4. A ball in the dirt. A ball in the dirt can be a tough call because the plate umpire will be straight-lined more on that play than any other. Adding to the difficulty of the call will be the sound of the ball hitting the ground directly before it may have hit the batter. If it looked like he was hit and he tried to move, he was probably hit.

5. Help from your partner. Getting help from your partner in hit-batter situations is a catch-22. Sometimes partners ride in like the cavalry and save the day. Other times they make the situation worse. That situation happens often enough that it should be covered in your pregame. Plus, what is said on the field can make all the difference in determining the crew's overall credibility.

Here is an approach to try: If after a pitch your partner is 100 percent sure that the pitch hit the batter, he should hesitate to see if you make the call. If after a few moments, you don't make a call, he should emphatically throw up both arms, call time and award the batter first. Try it. The key is that the base umpire must be sure.

If the base umpire doesn't make a call after your hesitation, you know he is not sure if the pitch hit the batter. You then know that you must use the other criteria in determining if you will award the runner first.

CASEPLAYS

Play 1: R2 is on second with one out. B3 is at bat with a 2-2 count. B3 checks his swing on an inside pitch, which hits B3's hand while it is in contact with the bat. Upon a proper appeal, the base umpire rules B3 swung at the pitch. What's the ruling if the ball goes into fair territory, goes to the backstop or goes directly to the catcher's mitt? **Ruling 1:** No batter hit by a pitch can be awarded first base if the pitch is ruled a strike. Because the ball is dead when the batter is hit by the pitch, it doesn't matter what happens to the ball afterward. Also, because the swing results in the third strike on the batter, he is out. Play continues with B4 at bat, R2 on second and two out.

Play 2: R1 is on first and is taking a big lead. F1 balks but delivers the pitch, which hits B2. What's the ruling? What's the ruling if there are other runners on base? **Ruling 2:** Under NFHS rules, the ball is dead when F1 balks. R1 is awarded second. If there were other runners on base, each would advance one base. In NCAA, if the batter and runner advance one base on the hit batter, the ball remains live and the balk is ignored. If there were runners on first and third or second and third, since the runners would not automatically advance on the hit batter, the balk is enforced and the pitch ignored. B2 would remain at bat with the same count.

Play 3: B1 is at bat with a three-ball, no strike count. The batter rolls his elbow into the strike zone and (a) the pitch hits B1 in the shoulder and would have been a ball, or (b) the pitch hits the batter in the elbow and was in the strike zone. In both cases, the batter made no other movement. **Ruling 3:** In (a) B1 is awarded first base as it was ball four, and in (b) B1 is charged with a strike.

Play 4: B1 is at bat with a two-ball, no strike count. The batter is fooled by the pitch and freezes in the box. The pitch hits B1 in the shoulder. The batter made no other movement. **Ruling 4:** B1 is awarded first base.

Play 5: On the third strike, B3 swings at and misses a pitch. The ball touches his arm or person. **Ruling 5:** B3 is out. The ball becomes dead immediately when it hits him.

Play 6: With R1 on first, B2 has two strikes. He swings at the next pitch, which touches him. R1 steals second. **Ruling 6:** B2 is out. The ball becomes dead when it hits B2 and R1 must return to first.

Play 7: B1 is at bat with a three-ball, two-strike count. He swings at the next pitch. The ball hits his right fist and, without contacting the bat, goes into foul territory. F2 retrieves the ball and throws to F3, who is covering first base. F3 tags B1 with the ball. **Ruling 7:** As soon as the ball hit the batter, it became dead. B1 is declared out. To have the play ruled a foul ball, the ball would have to have hit the bat of B1 before it touched his hand.

UNUSUAL PLAYS

Veteran umpire Jay Miner describes four of the more unusual hit batter plays he has encountered in his long career.

Situation 1: In a Little League game, the batter was struck in the ribs by an inside fastball. The player writhed in pain as he was attended to by the coach. The base umpire, judged the batter clearly "went for" the pitch that hit him. During the delay the base umpire discreetly informed his partner that he had "an attempt" to hit the ball by the batter. The mild-mannered plate umpire responded with, "Oh, no, no, no, no! Not on that play!" Obviously, he did not want a brouhaha by denying the injured batter first base.

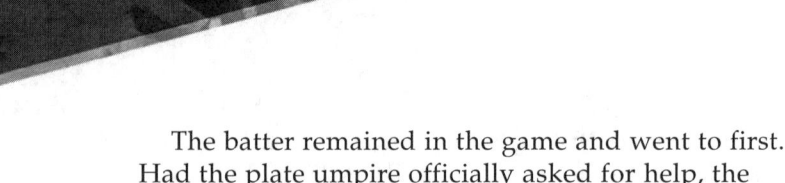

The batter remained in the game and went to first. Had the plate umpire officially asked for help, the base umpire said he would have called the pitch a strike.

Situation 2: A good hitter was "brushed" by a pitch. The umpire called, "Hit batter!" and directed the batter to first by motioning with his left arm. The batter stayed in the box and informed the umpire he was declining the hit batter award. His coach came out and supported his batter's choice of remaining at bat.

The umpire calmly told the batter and his coach that a hit batter situation is not an option play and that he must advance to first. Reluctantly, the batter went to first and his coach returned to the dugout.

Situation 3: The home team trailed by one run in the last of the seventh. With the bases loaded and two outs, the count was full on B1. The pitch bore in on B1 as he swung and sliced a foul ball behind the first-base dugout. B1 appeared to be in some discomfort as his coach came out to argue the pitch hit his batter.

The savvy umpire told the coach, "If you convince me your batter got hit, this game is over because I know he swung at the pitch!" The light in the manager's head went on. He practically ran back to the dugout. Oh yes, B1 struck out swinging on the next pitch to end the game.

Situation 4: In a varsity high school game, R1 was on first with no outs. B1 was up with two strikes. A tailing fastball nicked the bill of B1's helmet, tipped his bat and was caught by F2. F2 immediately fired to first and nailed R1 returning to the bag. The play happened so quickly, I never raised my arms to call time.

The plate umpire carefully recounted the sequence of events for the defensive coach. The umpire told the coach, "I know you aren't going to like this, but that isn't a double play."

The umpire continued, "I saw exactly what happened. The pitch touched the batter's helmet before anything else. That's a dead ball and a hit batter. Everything else is canceled. We've got runners on first and second and no outs. Too bad, because your catcher made a great play."

The coach pawed at the dirt with his foot and finally said, "You know, I think that's what happened myself." While walking away he said, "That's the damnedest thing I ever saw."

BRUSHBACKS VS. BEANBALLS

Determining the intent of a pitcher throwing an inside pitch often comes down to an educated guess, a gut instinct or an understanding of the mores of baseball.

Deciding whether a pitcher is intentionally throwing at the batter isn't always an easy call (PlayPic C). Umpires certainly don't need to read minds when a pitcher known for pinpoint control

A pitch near the batter's head should serve as a red flag that a pitcher may be intentionally throwing at a hitter.

decks a batter after giving up back-to-back home runs. But what about that pitch two or three inches inside, designed to make a batter crowding the plate back off? Do circumstances ever allow for a knockdown pitch? Should warnings ever be issued in the name of prevention, even when umpires are almost certain no infraction has been committed?

An umpire has three courses in potential beanball situations: no-call, warning or ejection. But the most important thing to remember when dealing with headhunting or even suspected headhunting is that, if you choose to issue warnings or ejections, the rulebook is on your side.

Moving the batter off the plate is not the same as headhunting. Few hitters are adept at hitting the inside pitch, and most inside pitches are thrown with the idea of exploiting the batter's weakness. That is especially true when wooden bats are used; an inside pitch will often lead to a broken bat and a weak ground ball.

A pitch a few inches off the plate that a batter can avoid with ease should be allowed provided it is not directed at the batter's head. Don't automatically succumb to pleas for ejections and warnings from the dugout. If pitchers know the brushback is unacceptable, the knockdown and beanball will likely never become a part of their repertoire.

An important consideration is the type of pitch and the game situation. Pitchers generally don't use changeups or breaking balls as "purpose pitches," nor do they throw at less-skilled hitters. With the count clearly in his favor, (0-2 or 1-2), a pitcher is more likely to try to get an out than try to make a statement. Most pitchers are sophisticated enough not to intentionally hit a batter late in a tied or close game, when a hit batsman would put the winning run on base, move the potential winning run into scoring position or drive in the lead run. In all but the rarest cases, such situations call for no action on the part of the umpire.

A warning may be appropriate if a pitcher hit or brushed back a batter to make a point. Such situations include but are not limited to batters who took an inordinately long time to circle the bases after hitting a home run the last time up, batters who attempt a sacrifice bunt late in a game with a big lead or players who attempted a take-out slide at a base in a previous inning. If those "message pitches" are aimed below the belt, an umpire may consider issuing a warning.

When you are absolutely certain the pitcher is deliberately throwing at the batter, the pitcher should be ejected immediately.

Well-coached hitters are taught to go into a defensive "rollaway" on an inside pitch. With that technique, the batter turns his front shoulder toward the catcher and away from the pitch. Consider the rollaway an attempt to get out of the way. Modern hitters are sometimes struck as they aggressively "dive in," a la Derek Jeter, to attack a pitch. Do not consider that movement as an attempt to intentionally get hit by a pitch. No one in his right mind wants to be hit with a 99 mile-per-hour fastball.

Beanballs can have devastating results. That's why they must be addressed before they escalate. Two of the most unsettling incidents in baseball history involve beanballs.

On Aug. 16, 1920, the only fatality as a direct result of a pitch in the history of Major League Baseball occurred when Yankee pitcher Carl Mays hit Cleveland shortstop Ray Chapman in the temple with a pitch. But in that pre-union, pre-sue-anybody-for-anything era, there was no outcry for players to wear batting helmets. In fact, it was 37 years before either major league addressed the issue of protective headgear.

According to *The Official Rules of Baseball Illustrated* by David Nemec, the AL ordered players to wear protective headgear starting with the 1957 season. Players were given the option of wearing helmets or plastic inserts inside their caps. Most players, trading the appearance of machismo over the protection offered by a helmet, chose the inserts.

The Society for American Baseball Research reports that inserts had actually come into vogue in 1941, when several members of the Brooklyn Dodgers began to wear them after Joe Medwick, Bill Jurges and Pete Reiser suffered serious head injuries.

Helmets with earflaps on the side of the helmet facing the pitcher didn't become prevalent until after Aug. 18, 1967, when perhaps the most famous beanball was thrown. California Angels pitcher Jack Hamilton threw a pitch that hit young Boston Red Sox star Tony Conigliaro on the left cheekbone. Conigliaro was knocked unconscious and was carried off the field on a stretcher. He was taken to Santa Maria Hospital in Cambridge, Mass., where it was determined he had suffered a fractured cheekbone, a dislocated jaw and a damaged retina.

According to *The Sporting News*, plate umpire Larry Napp issued no warnings and Hamilton was not ejected. Although several Red Sox screamed at Hamilton, the benches did not clear, no one charged the mound and there was no obvious reprisal. The box score shows Conigliaro as the only hit batsman in the game.

There is no evidence to suggest Hamilton threw at Conigliaro intentionally, although many Red Sox claim the pitch that hit Conigliaro was a wayward spitball. Hamilton's control could best be described as spotty; he walked 348 batters and hit 16 in 611 major league innings. Conigliaro suffered vision problems after the incident and was unable to fulfill the stardom for which he'd seemingly been destined.

Other players have had promising careers curtailed or cut short after being hit by pitches. Longtime Baltimore outfielder Paul Blair's average nosedived after he was hit. The same with Dickie Thon, a scrappy infielder who made a comeback after being hit in the eye but was never the same.

CHAP TER 6

Interference

Former Milwaukee Brewers second baseman Jim Gantner was famous for his malaprops. Gantner couldn't match Yogi Berra either as a player or as a butcher of the English language, but he did come up with some doozies.

In one game, Gantner fielded a ground ball and flipped to the shortstop in hopes of starting a double play. The runner went out of his way to slide away from the base and toward the shortstop, trying to prevent the twin killing.

Gantner saw the action and ran to the second base umpire. "Hey! Aren't you going to call that?" Gantner fumed. "That's construction! That's construction!"

The umpire was unmoved by Gantner's protest and made no call. He might have also chuckled at the mis-speak.

Had there been a call, of course, it would have been interference and not "construction." Interference is an act by the offense while obstruction is committed by the defense. If it's any consolation to Gantner, many people (including umpires) sometimes confuse the two.

THE RULES

According to NFHS rules, interference is an act (physical or verbal) by the team at bat which interferes with, obstructs, impedes, hinders or confuses any fielder attempting to make a play. It is interference when a runner creates malicious contact with any fielder, with or without the ball, in or out of the baseline; or if a coach physically assists a runner during playing action (PlayPic A).

It is illegal for a coach to physically assist a runner.

The NCAA rulebook defines interference as the act of an offensive player, umpire or non-game person who interferes with; physically or verbally hinders; confuses; or impedes any fielder attempting to make a play.

The college rulebook also provides five scenarios and the correct rulings:

• If the umpire declares the batter, batter-runner or a runner out for interference, all other runners shall return to the last base that was touched legally at the time of the interference, unless otherwise provide by these rules. The ball is dead.

• If the batter-runner has not touched first base at the time of interference, all runners shall return to the base last occupied at the time of the pitch. If there was an intervening play made on another runner, all runners shall return to the base last touched at the time of interference.

• If a fielder has a chance to field a batted ball, but misplays it and while attempting to recover it, the ball is in the fielder's immediate reach and the fielder is contacted by the base runner attempting to reach a base, interference shall be called.

• If a fielder has a chance to field a batted ball, but misplays it and must chase after the ball, the fielder must avoid the runner. If contact occurs, obstruction shall be called.

• If a fielder chases after a deflected batted ball ahead of a runner's arrival and is in the act of picking up the ball (fielding) when contact is made by an offensive player, interference is the call. If the fielder is chasing after the deflected batted ball and contact is made between the two players, it is obstruction and not interference.

In any interference situation in NCAA, if the batter or runner continues to advance after being put out, that act alone shall not be considered as confusing, hindering or impeding the fielders. Also, a runner who has been obstructed remains subject to team offensive interference penalties.

In addition to ruling whether an act by a coach, bat person, photographer or home-field attendant qualifies as interference, an NCAA umpire must judge whether that interference was intentional or unintentional. It is intentional interference if the coach or other person

fields, kicks or pushes a ball, regardless of possible motives. If the ball touches a coach or other person despite best efforts to avoid the contact or if the person doesn't see the ball coming, it is unintentional interference. In that case, the ball is live and in play.

Collisions between a runner and a fielder are not an everyday occurrence. When those do occur, the fielder usually has the right of way. The runner may also collide with the ball, and that usually results in an out as well.

RUNNER HIT BY BATTED BALL

If a runner is hit by a fair batted ball before it passes an infielder other than the pitcher, the ball is dead and the runner is out (PlayPic B). The batter-runner is

The runner is out if the batted ball strikes him before the ball passes an infielder other than the pitcher.

awarded first base and is credited with a hit. If all the infielders, on the runner's side of the infield, are playing in, a runner who is hit by a batted ball is not out unless he intentionally interferes.

A challenging scenario for umpires is when one infielder (most likely F3 or F5) is playing in front of the baseline and another infielder (most likely F4 or F6) is playing deep.

In NFHS and NCAA, the umpire must determine if the deeper (second) fielder might have been able to make a play. If so, the runner is out. If not, the ball remains in play.

If the first fielder did not have a legitimate chance to field the ball, the runner is out regardless whether another fielder could have fielded the ball.

Play 1: With R2 on second, B1 grounds the ball into the hole. F5, playing in front of the baseline, dives for the ball, which passes under his glove. The ball then hits R2. F6 had gone deep into the hole. **Ruling 1:** R2 is out if the umpire judges F6 might have been able to make a play. If F5 had touched (deflected) the ball and it then struck R2 (unintentionally on the part of the runner), it is live and in play despite the fact that another infielder might be in position to field the ball.

Play 2: With R2 on second and R3 on third, the infield is playing in. B1 grounds the ball into the hole about midway between F5 and F6. Neither fielder is within an arm's reach of the ball. The ball then hits R2. **Ruling 2:** The ball remains in play.

RUNNER HIT BY PITCHED BALL

There are two scenarios for a runner to be hit by a pitch. The first is a runner on third who is trying to steal home and the second is a batter-runner who makes contact with a dropped third strike.

If a runner tries to steal home and is hit by a pitch, the ball is immediately dead and the pitch is called a ball or a strike. All runners are awarded one base. In the rare circumstance that such a pitch were a strike, the batter would be out if it were strike three and the run would not score if strike three resulted in the third out.

After an uncaught third strike, the batter may not interfere with the catcher's fielding or throwing by stepping out of the batter's box or making any other movement that hinders the catcher's play. If while attempting to advance to first base, the batter-runner

intentionally deflects the ball, the batter-runner is declared out, the ball is dead and all runners return.

If he unintentionally deflects the ball, the ball is live and in play. NCAA rules further specify that if there are fewer than two outs and first base is occupied, the ball is dead and all runners return, unless the runner(s) are stealing on the pitch.

Play 3: With no runners on base, B1 swings and misses a pitch in the dirt for strike three. The catcher blocks the ball, which then rolls forward. As he leaves the batter's box, B1 kicks the ball into foul territory. B1 is safe at first. **Ruling 3:** The umpire must judge whether B1 intentionally kicked the ball. If so, B1 is out for hindering the catcher's attempt to field the ball; the ball is dead. If not, the play stands.

Play 4: B1 swings and misses a pitch in the dirt for strike three. B1 takes off for first and the catcher deflects the ball into him. B1 is safe at first. **Ruling 4:** The ball is live and in play. When a batter-runner has left the batter's box and is hit from behind by a ball deflected by the catcher, he should not be called out for interference.

RUNNER HIT BY THROWN BALL

Perhaps the most memorable incident of a runner hit by a thrown ball is that of Reggie Jackson in game four of the 1978 World Series between the Los Angeles Dodgers and New York Yankees. In the last of the sixth, the Yankees batted trailing, 3-0. With Jackson at first and Thurman Munson at second, Lou Piniella ripped a sinking liner to the left of Dodger shortstop Bill Russell. Russell dropped the ball, picked it up, stepped on second to force out Jackson and fired toward first. Jackson was only a few strides from first and froze in his tracks when the ball closed in on him. Without moving his feet, Jackson swiveled his right hip toward the ball. The ball struck Jackson in the right leg and bounced into short right field. Munson scored and Piniella was safe at first.

Dodger Manager Tommy Lasorda went ballistic as he vociferously argued with first-base umpire Frank Pulli that Jackson had intentionally interfered. But the call stood. The Yankees eventually won the game in the 10th inning.

Other than a batter-runner being hit by a thrown ball while outside the three-foot lane, in NFHS rules, a runner is guilty of interference only if he intentionally allows a thrown ball to hit him. In NCAA, the act does not have to be intentional.

Play 5: With R1 on first, B1 grounds sharply to F6, who tosses to F4 at second for the force. F4's throw to first hits a surprised R1, who was halfway to second. **Ruling 5:** In NFHS, the play stands. In NCAA, R1 is out for interfering with the throw.

RUNNER OUTSIDE LANE

The rules require the batter-runner to run the last half of the distance from home to first base within the three-foot lane. If the runner does not, there is no penalty unless, while the ball is being thrown to first

The batter-runner is out when struck by the throw when he is not in the three-foot lane.

base from the area of the plate, and in the umpire's judgment, he interferes with the fielder taking the throw at first base. Intent is not a factor. However, in NFHS, the quality of the throw is not a consideration in regard to three-foot lane interference. In NCAA, the throw must have a reasonable chance of retiring the runner in order for interference to be called.

RUNNER ON A BASE

A baserunner can be protected from interference by virtue of being on a base. The most common involves the runner's unintentional contact with (or hindrance of) a fielder during a batted ball. Two examples: a ground ball down the third-base line with a runner at third; R3 is trying to return and F5 is approaching the base to field the ball. The other is a fly ball that is coming down near a base. On those plays you must be sure that the contact or hindrance by the runner occurred after he returned to and was touching the base. If that's the way it happened, employ a strong safe signal punctuated with the "That's nothing!" declaration.

If the contact or hindrance by the runner happened before the runner got back, it is interference. Keep in mind that the runner is required to do what he can to avoid the fielder without leaving the base. If the runner does anything intentional to interfere, the intent supersedes the fact that he is on the base, and it is interference. With fewer than two outs, the interfering runner and the batter-runner are out; with two outs, the batter-runner is out.

INFIELD FLY CONSIDERATIONS

The less common of the two protections granted a runner on a base is an infield fly touching the runner on its descent. Again, you must be certain the runner returned to the base before the ball touched him. If he did, you'll signal time rather than safe since the ball is instantly dead. The batter-runner is out on the infield fly and the struck runner and any other runners remain on the bases they occupied at the time of the pitch.

TANGLE-UNTANGLE

It is incidental contact when a batter-runner starting toward first after bunting makes contact with the catcher, who is trying to go after the bunt. That rule came to the forefront in the 1975 World Series on a play involving batter-runner Ed Armbrister and catcher Carlton Fisk. Larry Barnett was working the plate that day. After the incidental contact, Fisk came free, grabbed the ball, threw wildly past second base, then claimed interference. Barnett correctly ruled that the contact (which occurred independent of the actual throw) was incidental.

There are a few other plays that may bring a fielder, runner and ball into the same vicinity.

For instance, if a batter bunts or chops a ball down the first-base line, a pitcher or first baseman (probably both) will be lurking in the area, waiting to see if the ball will go foul. Meanwhile, a batter-runner is running to first and meeting the requirement that he be in the running lane. If nothing extraordinary happens as batter-runner and fielder pass, even if there is slight contact or a momentary hindrance, it will likely be nothing more than incidental contact.

However, you'll have to use some common sense. Imagine the batter-runner running on the fair side of the running lane when he could have just as easily been running on the foul side. If he contacts the fielder just as the fielder grabs at the fair ball, it is probably interference. Likewise, if the fielder could have taken a position out of the way of the batter-runner, but instead intentionally moves into the runner's path to wait for the ball to go foul, it is likely obstruction. Note that the intent of each player should govern your judgment in those situations.

A related play involves a runner or batter-runner and fielder briefly jockeying when a fly ball is on its way up.

Once again, common sense must prevail. A fielder still has a reasonable chance to catch a fly ball despite brief contact or hindrance as the ball went up. In fact, the fielder was probably not exactly sure where to go, since the ball had not yet come close to the apex of its flight. Rather than interference, you must be more concerned with any hindrance of the fielder after the fly ball has reached its highest point.

Of course, an intentional action on the part of either the fielder or runner as the ball rises would bring interference or obstruction into the equation.

RUNDOWNS

During a rundown, a multitude of possibilities exist. Likewise, there will be occasions when incidental contact occurs. If a runner in a rundown goes out of his way to initiate non-malicious contact with a fielder who is not receiving a throw, you'll rule the contact incidental. It's not obstruction because the runner intentionally created the contact; it is not interference because the fielder is not fielding the ball. If a fielder is fielding a throw and the runner unintentionally contacts him just after he catches the throw — or just after he misses it — the contact is incidental. That's because interference involving a thrown ball generally requires an intentional act on the part of the runner. Under high school rules, if the fielder has the ball for a tag, the runner would be out for interference if he initiated a collision. The runner must slide or avoid the fielder and the contact may not be malicious. In NCAA play, if the runner could have avoided the collision but initiated it anyway, or intended to dislodge the ball or inflict harm, it is interference.

TWO OR MORE FIELDERS

If two or more fielders attempt to field a batted ball and the runner makes contact with either of them, the umpire shall determine which fielder is entitled to protection. The protected fielder cannot initially be guilty of obstruction; other fielders can be guilty.

Cases in which the initially protected fielder misplays a ball present a challenge for umpires. Imagine a play on which a fielder has a chance to field a batted ball, but misplays it. While attempting to recover it, if the ball remains within the fielder's immediate reach and the fielder is contacted by the baserunner attempting to reach a base, interference shall be called. If a fielder has a chance to field a batted ball, but misplays it and must chase after the ball, the fielder must avoid the runner. If contact occurs, obstruction shall be called.

Play 6: With a runner on first, B1 hits a ground ball to F4. The ball deflects off F4's glove and rolls back toward the mound. F4 (a) reaches and picks up the ball, (b) takes a step to reach the ball, or (c) takes several steps to reach the ball. In each case, R1 collides with F4. **Ruling 6:** In (a) and (b), it is interference by R1. A fielder is allowed "a step and a reach" after a batted ball is misplayed. In (c), it is obstruction by F4. Since he muffed the ball out of reach, he may not impede the runner.

BATTER INTERFERENCE
It is interference if a batter interferes with the catcher's fielding or throwing by leaning over home plate, steps out of the batter's box, makes any other movement which hinders actions at home plate (PlayPic D) or the catcher's attempt to play on a runner (PlayPic E), or

It is illegal for the batter to hinder action at home plate.

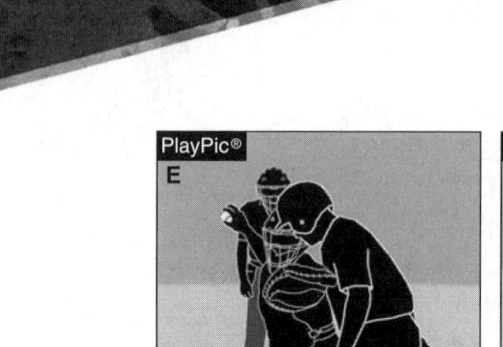

It is illegal for a batter to hinder the catcher's attempt to play on a runner or prevent him from fielding the ball on a dropped third strike.

fails to make a reasonable effort to vacate a congested area when there is a throw to home plate and there is time for the batter to move away. The batter-runner is out when he intentionally interferes with the catcher's attempt to field the ball after a third strike (PlayPic F).

When there are two outs, the batter is out. When there are not two outs and the runner is advancing to home plate, if the runner is tagged out, the ball remains live and interference is ignored. Otherwise, the ball is dead and the runner is called out. When an attempt to put out a runner at any other base is unsuccessful, the batter is out and all runners must return to bases occupied at the time of the pitch. If the pitch is a third strike and in the umpire's judgment interference prevents a possible double play (additional outs), two may be ruled out.

It is a delayed-dead ball when there is interference by a batter. When the batter interferes with the catcher attempting to play on a runner, if an out does not result at the end of the catcher's throw, the ball shall become dead immediately.

PlayPic® G

A coach may not hinder a fielder's attempt to catch a foul fly ball.

The batter is out when any member of the offensive team or coach interferes with a fielder who is attempting to field a foul fly ball. The ball becomes dead immediately (PlayPic G).

Play 7: With two outs, B3 strikes out, but the catcher drops the ball, which rebounds into B3's base path. As B3 begins running to first, B3 accidentally kicks ball. **Ruling 7:** B3 is not guilty of interference and the ball remains live, unless in the umpire's judgment B3 intentionally kicked the ball.

Play 8: With R2 going to third, B3 steps across home plate to hinder the catcher who is fielding the ball or throwing to third, or attempting to throw to third. **Ruling 8:** If R2 is tagged out despite the hindrance, the interference is ignored, and with less than two outs, the ball remains live. If R2 is not tagged out, B3 is declared out, and when there are less than two outs, the ball becomes dead immediately and all runners must return to the bases occupied at time of the pitch.

Play 9: With one out and R1 on first base, B3 swings and misses for (a) strike two, or (b) strike three and interferes with the catcher's throw to second base in an effort to put out advancing R1. **Ruling 9:** In NFHS, in (a), B3 is out and R1 is returned to first base. In (b), B3 has struck out. If, in the umpire's judgment, the catcher could have put out R1, the umpire can call him out also. If not, R1 is returned to first base. In NCAA, R1 is automatically out in both (a) and (b).

Play 10: With R1 on first base and R2 on second base, one out and two strikes on B4, R1 and R2 attempt a

double steal. B4 swings and misses the pitch and interferes with the catcher's attempt to throw out either R1 or R2. **Ruling 10:** If in the umpire's judgment the catcher could have made a putout on the runner(s) but cannot determine where the play was going to be made because of the nature of the interference, the umpire will then call out the runner nearest home plate, which is R2. R1 returns to first.

Play 11: With less than two outs, R2 on second and B3 at the plate, R2 attempts to steal third. In the process, B3, who bats right-handed, after swinging or not swinging at the pitch (a) makes no attempt to get out of the way of the catcher throwing to third, or (b) is unable to make an attempt to get out of the way of the catcher throwing to third. As a result, the catcher cannot make a play on the runner. Is B3 out, and must R2 return to second? **Ruling 11:** B3 is not guilty of interference in (a) or (b). B3 is entitled to his position in the batter's box and is not subject to being penalized for interference unless he moves or re-establishes his position after the catcher has received the pitch, which then prevents the catcher from attempting to play on a runner. Failing to move so the catcher can make a throw is not batter interference.

Play 12: With R3 on third, one out and two strikes on B4, B4 swings at and misses the pitch. The ball bounces off the catcher's glove into the air, where it is hit by B4's follow-through. The ball rolls to the backstop. B4 reaches first base safely and R3 scores. **Ruling 12:** The ball is dead immediately. B4 is out on the strikeout and R3 returns to third base. A batter is entitled to an uninterrupted opportunity to hit the ball, just as the catcher is entitled to an uninterrupted opportunity to field the ball. Once the batter swings, he is responsible for his follow-through.

Play 13: With no outs and F1 in the set position R3, who is on third base, attempts to steal home. F1 legally steps backward off the pitcher's plate and throws home.

B2 hits the ball. **Ruling 13:** Typically, batter's interference is a delayed-dead ball in order to give the defense an opportunity to make an out on the initial putout attempt. Since the batter hit the ball, the defense was not afforded an opportunity to make a play. Therefore, the ball is declared dead immediately. R3 is out because of B2's interference.

Play 14: With runners on first and third, R1 attempts to steal second. B3 interferes with the catcher. The catcher's throw is in time to retire R1. R3 takes advantage of the throw and scores. **Ruling 14:** Since the defense was able to retire the runner attempting to steal, the interference is ignored and the ball remains live. The run counts.

Play 15: With a runner on third base and one out, B3 walks. B3 takes several steps toward first base, stops and tosses the bat in front of home plate. The catcher throws the ball to third in an attempt to pick off the runner at third. The ball contacts the bat in mid-air and is deflected into dead-ball territory. **Ruling 15:** The ball is dead. Interference is declared on the batter. If the runner had been attempting to steal home, he would be declared out and the batter awarded first base on the base on balls. If the runner was attempting to return to third base on the play, the batter is declared out for the interference.

Play 16: B1 swings and misses a pitch for strike three. As the catcher is attempting to catch the pitch, B1 hits the catcher with the bat on the follow-through, hindering the catcher's attempt to catch the ball. **Ruling 16:** B1 is out for interference.

Play 17: B1 swings and misses a pitch for strike three. The ball ricochets from the catcher's mitt and rolls several feet down the first-base line in fair territory. As the catcher goes for the ball, B1 accidentally kicks or steps on the ball. **Ruling 17:** If, in the judgment of the umpire, B1 did not intentionally interfere, then the ball remains live and the play stands.

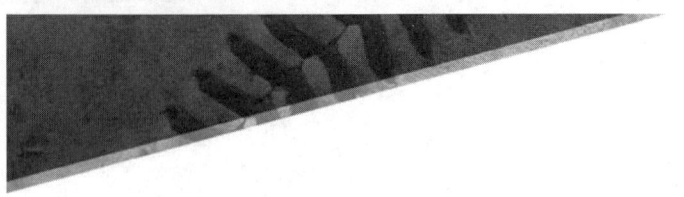

COLLISIONS WITH THE CATCHER

Although collisions can happen at other bases, most of them occur at the plate, as a runner is trying to score.

In both the NFHS and NCAA, the runner must take steps to avoid the collision, although more contact is permitted in the NCAA. In judging the collision, one key for umpires is to judge the location of the contact on the catcher. The base or plate is located at ground level. If the contact occurs above the waist (NFHS recommendation, NCAA rule), it is most likely an illegal collision. The runner can't be trying for the base while making contact above the waist.

In NFHS, the runner must legally attempt to avoid a fielder in the immediate act of making a play on him (having the ball is required). That does not mean that any contact will be penalized as interference. However, it puts the onus on the runner to do what he can to avoid contact. However, the runner may not jump, hurdle or leap over the fielder unless the fielder is on the ground. Diving over a fielder is not permitted at any time.

If contact occurs, the umpire must judge if the runner could have avoided contact. If he could, then interference shall be called. The runner is called out and all other runners return to the base occupied at the time of interference.

If the contact is malicious, the runner is also ejected from the contest.

In NCAA, the intent of the collision rule is to encourage runners and defensive players to avoid such collisions whenever possible.

When there is a collision between a runner and a fielder who clearly is in possession of the ball, the umpire shall judge the contact accordingly.

If the defensive player blocks the base (plate) or baseline with clear possession of the ball, the runner may slide into or make contact with a fielder as long as the runner is making a legitimate attempt to reach the base (plate). The runner must attempt to avoid a collision if he can reach the base without colliding.

If the runner's path to the base is blocked and he has made a legitimate attempt to reach the base without making contact above the waist, it is considered unavoidable contact, even if it appears to be violent in nature.

If the collision rule is invoked, the ball is dead immediately. If the contact was flagrant or malicious, the runner is ejected. He is also declared out if the contact occurred before touching the plate.

If the contact was flagrant or malicious after the runner had touched the base (plate), the runner will be ruled safe and ejected from the contest. The ball is immediately dead and all other base runners shall return to the last base touched at the time of the interference. If this occurs at any base other than home, the offending team may replace the runner.

UMPIRE INTERFERENCE

When an umpire inadvertently gets in the way of a play, he may end up having to eject a protesting coach. There is no means to completely rectify an umpire's transgression. In fact, in several situations the umpire's contact with the ball or player is ignored — no interference and play continues.

Situations in which an umpire may hamper play may be placed into four categories: batted ball, pitched or thrown ball, act of throwing and other player contact.

Batted ball. If a batted ball touches an umpire, the contact is ignored in certain situations and the ball remains live. In other cases, the ball is immediately dead.

PlayPic®
H

Umpire interference occurs when the catcher's attempt to throw is hindered.

If a fair batted ball touches an umpire in territory before passing an infielder other than the pitcher or touching any fielder, it is interference and the batter is awarded first base. The ball is dead and other runners advance only if forced.

On April 18, 1956, the Pittsburgh Pirates met the New York Giants at the Polo Grounds. Don Mueller was on first for the Giants as Alvin Dark batted. Dark hit a smash toward second baseman Johnny O'Brien. However, the ball struck second-base umpire Stan Landes who was working inside the diamond on the infield grass on the left heel. O'Brien fielded the ball and forced out Mueller at second. However, Landes correctly declared the ball dead and awarded Mueller second and Dark first.

However, if a fair ball touches an umpire after having passed an infielder other than the pitcher, or after having touched an infielder, including the pitcher, the ball remains live and in play.

Play 18: With the bases loaded and one out, B1 hits a line drive past F5. The fair ball hits the third-base umpire in the foot and deflects to F6. R3 scores, but B1 is thrown out at first. **Ruling 18:** The ball is live and in play; the run scores and B1 is out.

Umpire interference can be highly contentious. Every play is different; the umpire might block/deflect a sure base hit or a double play.

PITCHED OR THROWN BALL

Almost every pitch is thrown directly toward the plate umpire. Fortunately, 99 percent of the time, the ball is either batted, caught, deflected or blocked by the catcher. In some instances, the plate umpire serves as a hockey goalie and prevents a wild pitch or passed ball. No records are kept of umpire "saves." If a pitch touches an umpire, the contact is ignored and the ball remains live. The same applies to any thrown ball.

Play 19: The batter swings and misses for strike three. That pitch is missed by the catcher, as the batter starts for first. The ball strikes the umpire and is easily retrieved. The catcher fires to first to retire the batter. **Ruling 19:** The play stands.

Play 20: R1 attempts to steal second. The catcher's throw hits the base umpire, allowing R1 to reach second safely. **Ruling 20:** The play stands.

Play 21: With runners on first and third and one out, the batter hits a one-hopper to short. F6 throws to second to start the double play, but the throw hits the umpire. All runners are safe as one run scores. **Ruling 21:** The play stands.

ACT OF THROWING

In 1978, then-rookie NL umpire Eric Gregg bumped St. Louis Cardinals catcher Ted Simmons as Simmons attempted to throw the ball in the third inning in a game against the Los Angeles Dodgers. The interference call nullified a double steal by Davey Lopes and Bill Russell.

If an umpire hinders the catcher's throw, it is most likely interference (PlayPic H, previous page). If the hindrance occurs while the catcher is attempting to prevent a stolen base or pick off a runner, the ball is delayed dead. If the throw is prevented or does not retire the runner, interference is called. The ball becomes dead and runners return to their base. However, if the throw retires the runner, the interference is ignored.

Play 22: R1 is attempting to steal second. The catcher's arm accidentally strikes the umpire's mask. He hesitates briefly, then fires to second (a) in time, or (b) not in time, to retire the runner. **Ruling 22:** In (a), the contact is disregarded since the runner was retired. In (b), runners may not advance when the plate umpire interferes with the catcher's throw. R1 is returned to first.

Play 23: With a runner on first, the catcher receives the pitch and pivots to throw behind R1. He steps on the umpire's foot and throws wildly into right field. R1 advances to second. **Ruling 23:** The ball is dead and R1 returns. Since the catcher's throw did not retire the runner, it is interference.

If the hindrance occurs on an attempt to throw the ball back to the pitcher, the ball becomes immediately dead and no runners may advance.

Play 24: R1 on first. As the catcher is preparing to throw the ball back to F1, the catcher's throwing arm strikes the plate umpire. The throw rolls towards a dugout. Since no one was covering second, R1 takes off and makes it to second safely. **Ruling 24:** The ball is dead. Umpire's interference is ruled and R1 must return.

The hindrance may also occur while the catcher is fielding a batted ball or dropped third strike. In those situations, the play is treated the same as an attempt to prevent a stolen base and is delayed-dead.

Play 25: B1 strikes out on a pitch not caught in flight. As the catcher attempts to throw out B1, the umpire interferes. The resulting throw goes into (a) the dugout, or (b) right field. **Ruling 25:** In both (a) and (b), the ball is dead and the batter is out. Any other runners may not advance.

OTHER PLAYER CONTACT
If a runner or fielder collides with an umpire, play continues. Such contact will almost certainly bring a visit from the contacted player's coach.

Play 26: With two out and R2 on second, B1 hits a ground ball to the shortstop. F6's throw to first base is in the dirt and gets by F3. R2 rounds third base and is heading for home. Meanwhile, B1 rounds first base, collides with the base umpire, and is thrown out in a close play at second base. At the time of the out at second base, R2 was about five feet from home. **Ruling 26:** There is no interference. The out at second stands, R2 does not score.

CHAPTER 7

Obstruction

Obstruction is the act of a fielder who, while not in possession of the ball and not in the act of fielding the ball, impedes the progress of a runner.

An obstruction rule was in the Knickerbocker rules of 1857 and in the first official rules of 1876. Several modifications have been made over the years. The most recent changes have occurred in this century.

In 2008, the NFHS adopted changes as well. Fielders without the ball cannot "deny access" to a base (PlayPic A). To deny access, it must be a total denial — that is, the runner has no means of reaching

In NFHS, a fielder without the ball may not deny a runner access to a base.

the base without his running being altered. If a fielder without the ball blocks the portion of the base that the runner is trying to reach, it is not an infraction of the rule unless the base is totally blocked. There is no minimum required amount of access as long as a runner is given some access. Whether the base is totally blocked is a judgment call.

And for the 2011-12 NCAA season, the obstruction rule was revised to be more similar to what it was before the previous change in 2002, with one exception. A fielder is now permitted to block the base while in possession of the ball or in the "immediate act of fielding" a thrown ball.

As defined by the NFHS, obstruction is an act (intentional or unintentional, as well as physical or verbal) by a fielder, any member of the defensive team or its team personnel that hinders a runner or changes the pattern of play.

The NCAA definition of obstruction is more concise but is essentially the same in spirit and intent. Obstruction is the act of a fielder who, while not in the possession of the ball "or not in the act of fielding the ball," impedes the progress of any runner.

BLOCKING OFF A BASE

It is legal for the fielder to block the base because he has the ball.

In both codes, if the fielder is in possession of the ball, he is allowed to block the base and deny access (PlayPic B).

Play 1: F3 blocks R1 on a pickoff attempt. F3 does not have the ball. R1 (a) returns to first safely, or

(b) is out. **Ruling 1:** R1 is awarded second in both cases.

Play 2: R1 attempts to steal second. The throw is toward the first-base side of second base and pulls F6 off the base, into R1's path. When F6 and R1 collide, F6 (a) does, or (b) does not have possession of the ball. **Ruling 2:** In (a), R1 is out if tagged; in (b), it may be obstruction in NFHS, but is definitely not obstruction under NCAA rules. Since F6 did not have the ball under NFHS rules, he cannot deny access to the base. If his action in going for the thrown ball denies complete access to the runner, then obstruction is called. Under NCAA rules, since the fielder is in the act of fielding a thrown ball, the play stands.

Play 3: R1 attempts to steal second. As F4 covers, the throw goes into center field. As R1 rounds second, he collides with F6, falls down and returns to second. **Ruling 3:** That's obstruction. In NFHS, R1 is awarded third as all obstruction carries a mandatory one-base award. In NCAA, while obstruction is called, there is no automatic award since the runner is not being played upon.

In NCAA play, if a fielder is about to receive a thrown ball and the throw is close enough to the fielder that he must occupy his position to catch the ball, he may be considered in the act of fielding. That is strictly an umpire judgment call. It most often occurs on close plays at the plate. The NFHS revision from 2009 requires the fielder to have the ball.

Play 4: F2 is at the plate awaiting the throw as R3 is attempting to score. R3 slides into the plate and is prevented from touching it by F2's blocking position. The ball then arrives and F2 tags R3. **Ruling 4:** In NFHS, if the umpire determines that R3 was denied access to the base, obstruction is called and R3 is awarded home. In NCAA, the umpire must decide if F2 was in the "immediate" act of fielding a throw at the time of the contact.

Contact with a fielder who is about to receive a throw may happen other than at the plate.

Play 5: With R3 on third, F1 attempts a pickoff and gets R3 in a rundown. F5 throws to F2, who starts to run R3 back toward his base. F2 releases the ball, which is in flight toward F6 at third base. Just after the ball is released, the runner crashes into (a) F6, or (b) F5, who was in the baseline. In both cases R3 is subsequently tagged while off the base. **Ruling 5:** In (a), R3 is most likely out. In order for it to be called obstruction, F6 would have had to deny total access to the base. In NCAA, the umpire would have had to determine that F6 was not in the immediate act of fielding the ball. If obstruction is ruled, R3 is awarded home under both rules codes. In (b), F5 is guilty of obstruction and R3 is awarded home.

Play 6: R3 is attempting to score. R3 slides legally into F2. The contact causes the ball to pop out of F2's mitt, but he recovers the ball and tags R3. **Ruling 6:** R3 is out. The catcher has a right to block the plate when he has the ball.

ADVANCING BEYOND AWARDED BASE

If the runner advances beyond the base he would have been awarded, he does so at his own risk. If he is subsequently tagged out, the umpire must determine whether the obstruction had any bearing on the out. If not, the out stands despite the obstruction.

One prime example occurred in the 2003 AL playoffs. Oakland's Miguel Tejada was obstructed by Boston third baseman Bill Mueller. However, Tejada trotted home, assuming he was going to be awarded the base. Instead, he was tagged out. There was no base award since there was no play being made on him. When the out stood, Tejada and the Oakland staff couldn't believe it, but the ruling was correct.

BATTER-RUNNER OBSTRUCTED BEFORE REACHING FIRST

If a catcher and the batter-runner contact each other when the catcher is fielding the ball, there is generally no violation if they are both "where they are supposed to be and doing what they are supposed to do." Neither interference nor obstruction is called if neither player attempts to alter the play; the contact is considered incidental. Flagrant contact on the part of either player is a violation and the appropriate call — interference or obstruction — should be made.

Play 7: Right-handed B1 bunts the ball down the first-base line. He starts for first as F2 starts to field the ball. They brush shoulders as both proceed toward first. **Ruling 7:** The play stands. The contact is incidental.

Play 8: B1 tops a ball down the first-base line. B1 is advancing toward first base while F2 comes from behind to field the fair ball. F2 inadvertently trips B1, retrieves the ball and tags him. **Ruling 8:** When the batter-runner is tripped from behind, obstruction should be called. B1 is awarded first base.

Other situations in which the batter-runner may be obstructed before reaching first base and an award will be made include a ground ball to an infielder, a fly ball or line drive to an infielder that is dropped before the batter-runner reaches first base and a ball hit to the outfield. Those are delayed dead-ball situations.

There are also situations in which the batter-runner may be obstructed before reaching first base and not be entitled to any award. The principle is that the obstruction had no bearing on the result of the play. Examples include a fly ball or line drive that is caught (the out stands), and a foul ball that is not caught (the foul ball stands).

Play 9: With two outs, B1 flies to center field. The pitcher, believing the half inning is over, sprints for the first-base dugout and obstructs B1 before he has touched first. The fly ball is then (a) caught, or (b) not caught, with B1 thrown out at second on a close play. **Ruling 9:** In (a), B1 is out. The obstruction had no effect on the play. In (b), the umpire will award B1 second base.

Play 10: With a runner on first, B1 singles to right. Both the ball and R1 are on their way to third when F3 "accidentally" trips B1 who, after touching first, is on his way back to the base. There is no subsequent throw to first and speedy R1 beats the throw to third. **Ruling 10:** In NFHS, an obstructed runner must be awarded one base, no matter how incidental the contact might be. B1 is awarded second. In NCAA, since no play was being made on B1, he is not awarded the next base. B1 remains at first.

NO PLAY ON RUNNER

If a play on the runner is not in progress, the codes agree that obstruction is a delayed-dead ball. Situations in which obstruction may occur while the runner is not being played on include the batter-runner rounding first on a base hit while the ball is in the outfield and runners rounding second or third on a hit to the outfield.

An example of obstruction.

Play 11: With R2 on second, B1 hits into the gap. R2 rounds third, collides with F5, who is watching the play (PlayPic C), and is knocked to the ground. R2 gets up and advances past third and about halfway home. He then decides to retreat to third as the ball is relayed home. **Ruling 11:** R2 is awarded home. Even though he advanced one base beyond the obstruction, he would have scored without the obstruction.

CATCHER'S OBSTRUCTION

PlayPic®
D

The ball is delayed dead when catcher's obstruction occurs.

When the defensive player involved is the catcher, it is common parlance to refer to that act as "catcher's interference." However, it is technically obstruction. The ball is delayed dead when catcher's obstruction occurs. The violation is illustrated in PlayPic D.

It is obstruction if the catcher (or any other fielder, for that matter) interferes with the batter's swing or prevents the batter from striking at a pitched ball. The college rule specifies that catcher's interference on a batter should be called only on the batter's actual swing to hit the pitch. If a batter taking practice swings hits the catcher or the catcher's mitt during the backswing, the umpire immediately should call time but not enforce a penalty.

Under both codes, if a play follows the obstruction, the team at bat may elect to ignore the interference and accept the play. NFHS rules spell out that the decision must be made before the next pitch (legal or illegal), before the award of an intentional base on balls or before the infielders leave the diamond.

In both codes, if the batter reaches first base and all other runners advance at least one base, the obstruction is ignored. Any runner attempting to steal on a catcher's

obstruction with the batter's swing shall be awarded the base the runner is attempting to reach. If a runner is not attempting to steal on the catcher's obstruction, the runner is only entitled to the next base if he is forced to advance because the batter is awarded first base.

Play 12: R2 is on second and is stealing on the pitch. F2 tips the bat of B2, who swings and misses. F2's throw to third results in R2 being called (a) out, or (b) safe. **Ruling 12:** In (a), R2 is awarded third base and the batter is awarded first base. In (b), the batter is awarded first base. Since R2 was stealing at the time of the pitch, he is awarded third base.

Play 13: The bases are loaded with one out when F2 obstructs the batter's swing. B4 hits a pop fly and the umpires correctly declare the infield-fly rule. The ball is caught. **Ruling 13:** B4 is awarded first base on the obstruction and each runner is forced to advance one base as a result.

Play 14: R3 tries to score on a suicide squeeze bunt. F2 obstructs B2's swing. **Ruling 14:** That is catcher's obstruction. R3 is awarded home and B2 is awarded first base.

Play 15: R2 occupies second when B8 is obstructed by F2. B8's swing results in a grounder to F6, who throws B8 out at first base. R2, who was not stealing on the pitch, attempts to advance to third. F3's throw to third is in time to retire R2. **Ruling 15:** Because of the obstruction, B8 is awarded first base. R2 is returned to second base because he was not stealing on the pitch and he is not forced to advance by virtue of B2 becoming a runner.

Play 16: With R3 on third and no outs, B6 swings and that swing is interfered with by F2. B6 still manages to hit a fly ball to center field. R3 tags and scores. **Ruling 15:** Because of the obstruction, B6 is awarded first base and R3 is returned to third. The offensive team may elect to accept the result of the play (R3 scores, B6 out) instead of the interference penalty. The option on catcher's interference as described is the only play in baseball where the offense may elect to ignore a penalty.

VERBAL OBSTRUCTION

Only NFHS rules provide a penalty for verbal obstruction. An example: With R1 on first, the team at bat attempts a hit-and-run. With R1 running, the pitch gets away from F2. As R1 approaches second, F6 tells him the batter hit a foul ball. F2 recovers the ball and throws to F4, who tags R1. In that scenario, when the umpire in a high school game hears F6 give R1 false information, he should immediately call time and award R1 one base on the verbal obstruction. If R1 had reached second when F6 yelled and R1 is tagged between second and third, R1 is awarded third. If R1 has yet to reach second, he is awarded second.

FAKE TAG

Another rule unique to NFHS involves a fake tag. A fake tag is an act by a defensive player without the ball that simulates a tag.

A fake tag is considered obstruction. When a runner is obstructed while advancing or returning to a base by a fielder who, without the ball, fakes a tag, the umpire shall award the obstructed runner and each other runner affected by the obstruction the bases they would have reached, in his opinion, had there been no obstruction. If the runner achieves the base he was attempting to acquire, the obstruction is ignored. The obstructed runner is awarded a minimum of one base beyond his position on base when the obstruction occurred.

At the end of playing action following a fake tag, the umpire shall issue a warning to the coach of the team involved and the next offender on that team shall be ejected.

Play 17: B1 is moving toward second base on a hit to right field. F6, who does not have the ball in his possession, fakes a tag on B1. **Ruling 17:** That is ruled obstruction, and B1 is awarded second base or if, in the umpire's judgment, the runner could have advanced farther had obstruction not occurred, the umpire could award additional bases.

Play 18: B1 is returning to first base and F3, who does not have the ball, fakes a tag on B1. **Ruling 18:** In both cases it is ruled obstruction, and B1 is awarded second base or if, in the umpire's judgment, the runner could have advanced farther had obstruction not occurred, the umpire could award additional bases.

Play 19: R1, who is on first base, attempts to steal second base. F2 (a) does not make a throw, or (b) throws the ball into center field. In both cases F6 fakes a tag on R1. **Ruling 19:** In (a), R1 is awarded second base on the obstruction call. In (b), the umpire shall call a delayed-dead ball and award bases that in his judgment the runner would have obtained had the obstruction not occurred. The umpire shall issue a warning to the defensive coach for F6 faking a tag.

TIPS AND TECHNIQUES

In determining the base a runner will be awarded, it is appropriate for the umpire to consider the position of the ball, the runner and the fielder at the moment the obstruction occurs. However, the ultimate decision in awarding bases shall not be made until all play has ceased and shall be based on the principle that the obstructed runner is entitled to the base he would have reached had no obstruction occurred.

Failure to give the safe signal and say, "That's nothing," may be the most common rule-enforcement mistake on the field. The safe signal and accompanying verbal call should be used when interference, obstruction or some other violation or dead ball has been a possibility, but does not occur. Another is what some refer to as "incidental contact."

Many umpires fail to see the importance of such signaling. During certain plays, baserunners and fielders alike are protected from what otherwise would be rules violations.

MECHANICS

Depending on the level of play and the situation, a variety of signals are used when obstruction occurs. In NFHS, the umpire denotes the obstruction with the delayed-dead ball signal by extending his left arm parallel to his shoulders with a clinched fist. The umpire will also make a verbal call. When play ceases, the umpire calls time and awards bases as necessary.

In NCAA, when a play is being made on an obstructed runner, the umpire extends both arms overhead and calls time. The umpire then points laterally at the obstruction and makes a verbal call.

If no play is being made on the obstructed runner, the umpire steps assertively toward the play, points aggressively and makes a verbal call. Play continues until all activity ceases or the obstructed runner is tagged.

SUMMARY

As a matter of review, let's look at the key points of each topic one final time

APPEALS
- The NFHS permits a dead-ball verbal appeal.
- In NCAA, the ball must be live and either the base or runner must be tagged. Dead-ball appeals are not permitted.
- Appeal plays are not automatically force plays. If the runner was forced to advance to the base being appealed, then it is a force play and no runs may score if that was the third out. If the runner was not forced, the appeal is a time play.

BALKS
- Simply "deceiving the runner" is not a balk. A balk is when a pitcher illegally deceives a runner.
- In NFHS, all balks are immediate dead balls. Nothing that happens after a balk matters.
- In NCAA, balks remain live if the pitcher immediately throws or pitches.

BATTING OUT OF ORDER
- Only the defense can appeal batting out of order once the improper batter has completed his time at bat.
- The proper batter is always the batter called out on a successful appeal.
- The NFHS permits outs on a ball batted by an improper batter to stand, such as on a double play. In NCAA, a batting-out-of-order appeal supercedes all other outs on the batted ball.

CHECKLIST

FORCE-PLAY SLIDE RULE
- The rule is a safety rule as much as it is an interference rule.
- The result of a violation is the runner and the batter-runner are out and all other runners return to the base occupied at the time of pitch.
- The plate umpire is primarily responsible for the call in the two-umpire system.

HIT BY PITCH
- A batter is not allowed to intentionally permit himself to get hit.
- When a batter is hit by a pitch, the ball is dead immediately.
- The hands are not part of the bat. A ball that hits the hand has hit the batter.

INTERFERENCE
- Offensive interference is almost always an immediate dead ball.
- A runner who avoidably collides with a catcher is guilty of interference.
- Almost always, the runner must yield to a fielder who is fielding a batted ball.

OBSTRUCTION
- In NFHS, an obstructed runner is always awarded one base from his position at the time of obstruction.
- If, in the umpire's judgment, a runner advanced farther than he would have without the obstruction, he does so at his own risk.
- Only NFHS considers a fake tag to be automatically obstruction.

magazine
REFEREE
Is **Better** than ever

⊙ **12 ISSUES OF *REFEREE* MAGAZINE FOR JUST**
$29.95

Every issue is packed with the latest officiating news, up-to-date rules information and interpretations, special features on relevant issues like training, industry hot topics, and interviews with the top personalities in officiating.

In each issue of *Referee*:

- Journal of Record Reports
- In-depth Articles and Features
- Rules, Mechanics and Techniques
- Caseplays
- Interviews
- *NEW* **All Sports** section – containing game management, philosophies, tips and techniques that apply to <u>all sports</u>.

Don't delay – **Save 64%** off the cover price and get the next 12 issues for only $29.95*!

Name _____

Address _____

City _____ State _____ Zip _____

Email _____

Please check one of the following boxes:

☐ Renewal ☐ New Subscriber ☐ Payment Enclosed ☐ Bill Me Later

Send to: 2017 Lathrop Ave.
Racine, WI 53405

⊙ Go to **www.referee.com/promo/P05SUBR** or call **1-818-487-4549**

Please make sure to mention Promotion code: **P05SUBR** when ordering.

*U.S. Only